A Faith for the Future

T0268906

in the
**Church's
Teachings
for a
Changing
World** series

JESSE ZINK

Morehouse Publishing
NEW YORK

Morehouse Publishing, 19 East 34th Street, New York, NY 10016

Morehouse Publishing is an imprint of Church Publishing Incorporated.
www.churchpublishing.org

Cover design by Laurie Klein Westhafer
Interior design and typesetting by Beth Oberholtzer Design

Library of Congress Cataloging-in-Publication Data

Zink, Jesse A.
    A faith for the future / Jesse A. Zink.
        pages cm. — (The church's teachings for a changing world series ; Volume 3)
    Includes bibliographical references.
    ISBN 978-0-8192-3259-5 (pbk.) — ISBN 978-0-8192-3260-1 (ebook)
1. Episcopal Church—Doctrines. I. Title.
    BX5930.3.Z56   2016
    230'.3—dc23
                                                           2015031355

Printed in the United States of America

Contents

Introduction

For two thousand years, people have sought to make sense of the life, death, and resurrection of Jesus of Nazareth, an itinerant Jewish teacher who was remembered by his followers as the Messiah, the Christ, the Anointed One of God. From the earliest apostles, through desert monastic communities, into medieval cathedrals and academic theologians at the center of worldly power, and on to the present day, through division, discord, and schism, the followers of Jesus have sought to put into thoughts and words what we understand about the God of Jesus Christ. This is **theology**: reason or speech (*logos*) about God (*theos*). Whether explicit or not, all followers of Jesus have theological beliefs. These beliefs undergird the life of our Christian communities.

Christians in The Episcopal Church inherit this long tradition of theology. This rich and fertile history is one of the reasons I am an Episcopalian. But I also know that we look toward a future church whose outlines are uncertain. Many people long to be connected with the transcendent, with the divine, and with one another, but fewer and fewer seem interested in organized religion or, more disturbingly, can see how it is relevant to their lives. Economic growth and consumption dominate our lives, upending existing relations, the environment, and the global economy. The only thing that seems for sure is that the situation is changing rapidly.

The tradition of faith Episcopalians inherit is linked with the future church emerging in our midst. Our theological heritage is not something to be confined to a dusty back room; it is to be put at the center of our life together, where these ancient ideas continue to be relevant to our work for a future church. Grounded in theology, Episcopalians can move into the future to which God calls us.

Theology and Mission, Mission and Theology

Not everyone shares these ideas. Many people assume theology is the preserve of a special elite. Whether priests in their pulpits or academics in their ivory towers, it is easy to think theological reflection is reserved for a minority of Christians and, in some cases, is only dubiously linked to the life of the church.

Such ideas would have struck early Christians as decidedly odd. For instance, in the course of spreading the gospel message far and wide, Peter and Paul, two early followers of Jesus, encountered the vexing question of what role non-Jewish converts could take in the nascent Christian community. The issue generated intense theological controversy, recorded in the Acts of the Apostles and in Paul's letters to various Christian communities. At the heart of the church's life, people were engaging in theological reflection that led to a new understanding of the expansiveness of God's love made known in Jesus Christ.

Peter and Paul remind us of another important aspect of theology. Theology starts with telling other people about Jesus—what we call **evangelism**. Paul never would have taught about how Jesus Christ is for all people if he had kept that good news to himself. Likewise, in the nineteenth and twentieth centuries, European missionaries in foreign lands encountered new practices and customs, which inspired them to reflect on what was central to the Christian gospel and what were merely cultural add-ons. It was only when I began to work as a missionary of The Episcopal Church in South Africa that I found it necessary to seriously reflect on what I believed and how I saw God's love at work around me. When people ask me how they explain their faith to a non-Christian friend who teases them for going to church, that is a question that needs a theological answer. It is at the frontiers of our faith communities and the edges of our comfort zones that we find the most fertile ground for theological reflection.

Theology is best done—indeed, only done—when it is linked to the active work of telling others about the good news of Jesus Christ. Evangelism—or **mission**, a related word that refers to our being sent to share this good news—goes hand in hand with theology. Each informs the other. In theological reflection, we are emboldened to go forward in mission. In mission, we discover material for theological reflection. The theology of our future church is inseparable from our mission in a changing world.

Sources for Theology

Outlining a theology of The Episcopal Church is not straightforward. Other denominations have clear statements of faith. Episcopalians subscribe to an ecumenical set of creeds that ground the life of the church. We have important theologians, past and present, whom earlier volumes in this series have discussed (see Volume 1, *The Episcopal Way*, and Volume 2, *The Episcopal Story: Birth and Rebirth*). Over the centuries since the English Reformation, people like Richard Hooker, F. D. Maurice, Michael Ramsey, and Rowan Williams in England; William Porcher DuBose, William Stringfellow, and Kathryn Tanner in the United States; and many others around the world have influenced Anglican and Episcopal theology, but none has an exclusive shaping power.

Episcopalians are fond of saying our theology is rooted in prayer. A famous dictum is *lex orandi, lex credendi*, which literally translates as "the law of praying is the law of believing." More loosely, we can say, "praying shapes believing." Episcopalians often suggest that if you want to know what we believe, come pray with us.

Long before I became a missionary or thought about ordination, I was a child growing up in church. Every week I was wrapped up in Episcopal liturgies—the forms of worship and prayer we use—that began to teach me how we reason about and offer worship to the God of Jesus Christ. The Book of Common Prayer that contains those liturgies, therefore, is a basic source for this book.

Another important source of Episcopal theology is the creeds that emerged in the first few centuries of the church's life. A **creed** is a statement of belief, from the Latin word "credo" meaning "I believe." As part of our Sunday worship, Episcopalians recite the Nicene Creed. It is the product of a series of meetings among some early Christian leaders who came together to spell out how they understood the good news of Jesus Christ. The first of these meetings was held at Nicaea in what is now Turkey, starting in 325. The meetings were contentious. Some who were invited chose not to participate. Others who did participate were condemned as heretics. Yet over time their work came to shape the church as it developed in the Roman Empire, continental Europe, and eventually in North America. (Separate but related strands of theological reasoning shaped Christians farther east, leading to distinct traditions as far as India and China within only a few centuries of Christ's death. But the focus of this book is The Episcopal Church, whose heritage is predominantly western.) By reciting the Nicene Creed on Sundays, Episcopal congregations are a living link to this tradition.

Underlying both the liturgies of the prayer book and the creeds is, of course, the **Bible**, the record of God's dealings with the world. The Bible is the root of theology in The Episcopal Church. It contains, Episcopalians believe, "all things necessary to salvation."[1] This does not mean everything in the Bible is necessary for

---

1. Bishops, priests, and deacons affirm this when they are ordained (BCP, 513). The phrase is part of the four affirmations in the Chicago-Lambeth Quadrilateral of 1886 and 1888, which sets out the core beliefs of The Episcopal Church in seeking ecumenical relations with other Christians (BCP, 877).

salvation. Nor does it mean the Bible speaks with a single voice on every question. Different gospels highlight different aspects of Jesus's ministry. In places, Paul's letters express one approach to theology while James's letter expresses another. But the affirmation that the Bible contains all things necessary for salvation means Episcopalians can tell a complete story about the workings of God and its relation to our lives based on Scripture. And so, in thinking about theology, mission, and the life of the church, we will turn repeatedly to Scripture, prayer, and the creeds.

The Good News

The New Testament speaks of growth in the Christian faith. It's a good metaphor. I've known Christians who are mature in the faith. And I've known others who are younger, still developing. This status doesn't necessarily correspond with one's age. In any community, different people from different walks of life will be at different stages along a theological journey. It's a journey of allowing God to speak to, in, and through us.

Think of this book as a tool to help you grow a little bit further in faith, and to outline the beliefs that make up the Christian faith as it is understood in The Episcopal Church. It is not a work of systematic theology or a treatise on doctrine, nor is it the definitive understanding of theology in The Episcopal Church. Instead, this book offers a reading of Episcopal liturgy, the creeds, and the Bible in a way that responds to the nature of the world in the twenty-first century.

Put differently, I want in this book to share the good news of Jesus Christ and to help others discover more fully how The Episcopal Church understands it. The earliest Christians believed that in the life, death, and resurrection of Jesus Christ, the God who created the world and called Israel to be God's people had proclaimed something new, different—and good. They called this **gospel**, or *evangelion*, meaning "good news." What God did in and through Christ was not only new, it was genuinely, uniquely, wonderfully good. Whatever else we want to say about Christian theology, at its core we will find something that is both good and new.

We can summarize that gospel in a single word: grace. Grace is the love of God made known in Jesus Christ. It is a love like no other. It is a love that transforms our very being. It is a love that we cannot earn; through no action of our own can we become worthy of it. At the most basic level, God's orientation toward the world is deeply and profoundly one of love. This good news speaks as powerfully to a twenty-first-century world as it did to a first-century world. Followers of Christ have to hear, listen, and discern that good news in our own contexts, so that we can then share it with others.

In the twenty-first century, there is constant pressure to communicate in ever shorter sentences and thoughts. The length of a tweet—140 characters—has become the new normal. But for Christians who have always believed in a core gospel, tweeting is no problem. So here is one way to summarize the good news of Jesus Christ in a tweet: "You are loved with a love unlike any else that leads to a life unlike any else—now go, show that love & life to others. #grace #gospel" (That's 134 characters, actually.)

As with many tweets, huge oceans of meaning lie under each word. It is in this ocean of theology and mission that this book swims.

TO PONDER

- Theology is thinking about God. What moments in your life have led you to think about God? In other words, in what ways are you already a theologian?

- What do you make of the concept "*lex orandi, lex credendi*"? Do you pray, in any way? If so, how does that shape or reflect what you believe about God?

- How would you summarize the content of the Christian good news in 140 characters or less?

Chapter 1

God

On Sundays in most Episcopal churches, just after the sermon, the priest invites the congregation to stand and "affirm our faith in the words of the Nicene Creed." The people rise and say together a string of sentences that begins, "We believe in one God, the Father Almighty, maker of heaven and earth."

This is the **Nicene Creed**, the product of a series of church councils in the fourth and fifth centuries. Over many years, early Christian bishops and leaders came together to sort out (and re-sort out) some of the most basic theological beliefs about the God they believed to be **Triune**—literally, three-in-one. They structured the creed to reflect the three divine persons who make up one God: the Father, the Son, and the Holy Spirit. We'll return to these relationships in later chapters. This opening affirmation about God orients the Christian faith.[2]

There is a God. This God is a being who is both uniquely and definitively other to our human existence, and at the same time intimately involved in our lives. God is both the Almighty, Creator

---

2. The Nicene Creed can be found on pages 326–327 and 358–359 of the Book of Common Prayer. Because it is central to much of Christian theology, it is also reprinted on pages 89–90 of this book.

of all that is, seen and unseen, and also so lovingly attentive to us that we relate to this God with the familiarity of a parent.

Moreover, the Christian God is the "one" God. In the cultural ferment of the Roman Empire, there was a raft of competing religious traditions, all demanding fidelity to their particular god or gods. But Christians asserted faithfulness to a particular God, the God who was revealed in and through Jesus Christ. The God of Jesus Christ was not new. Jesus's God was the God of the Jewish people, the God known as **Yahweh**, who had called a people named Israel into being and sent them into the world to make God's glory known. When early Christians affirmed that they, too, believed in this "one God," they affirmed that the history of God's dealings with the people of Israel in the Old Testament was about them as well.

Creator and Covenant-Maker

The collection of laws, historical accounts, prophetic testimonies, poetry, proverbs, and much else that make up the Old Testament offer a place to begin thinking about the one God of the Christian faith. The Old Testament teaches us that God is not distant and removed. Instead, God acts in the world.

The first of these actions is creation. Out of nothing, God created the earth, the heavens, and all that is in them (Genesis 1–2). Nothing forced God to create. God created out of God's great love. And when God created, God looked at this new creation and said it was good. God acts out of love and God's love results in deep and profound goodness. Humans are made in the image of this God, which means we are made to be loving, good, and creative forces, too.

God also acts to create **covenants** with the people God has created. From ancient ancestors like Noah and Abraham and Sarah, to Moses, David, and others, God makes agreements. While the details are different, the basic idea of covenant is summed up in what God says through the prophet Jeremiah: "you shall be my people, and I will be your God" (Jeremiah 30:22; also Exodus 6:7 and Leviticus 26:12). God lovingly chooses a particular group of people through whom God will act in the world, first by promising Abraham that he will become the father of a multitude of descendants. That promise is realized in the Hebrew people who settle in Egypt, and yet again when Moses leads them out of Egypt with the promise of a new land and a better home. By worshipping God and working to bring about the kind of society God desires, these chosen people will be blessed by God.

Christians adopt this belief in the particularity of God's people. The first letter of Peter calls Christians "a chosen race, a royal priesthood, a holy nation" (1 Peter 2:9). Such language doesn't seem to square with the belief that all humans are created in the image of God. How are we all equal if some people are chosen and others are not? God chooses people not simply to bless them and set them apart from others, but so that through them all people may be blessed and know God's love. God calls a people because God needs a whole community of people to make God's blessing known. That tells us something important about God: God cannot be followed alone.

Yet the story doesn't always unfold smoothly. God's chosen people routinely fail to uphold their covenant with God. Their communities fracture and split. The world does not experience God's blessing through them. Through judges, kings and queens, and prophets, God continually calls God's people back to their covenant. This process culminates in the **Incarnation**, the birth of Jesus Christ in Bethlehem. In Christ, God takes flesh—the literal meaning of incarnate—and acts in the world in an entirely new way. We will take up this topic in later chapters, but for now notice this: in God's action in Jesus Christ, we learn that God's love is now both particular and universal. It is no longer just a chosen nation that is called by God. Through Jesus Christ, membership in that chosen nation is now open, potentially, to all people everywhere.

Our Father?

When Episcopalians offer the opening words of the Nicene Creed in worship—"We believe in one God, the Father Almighty, maker of heaven and earth"—we are affirming the creative power of God, the goodness and love of God, and the covenant and calling of God. But these words pose complications as well. In the Nicene Creed, Christians call God "Father." Some faithful Christians struggle with this language. If God is so completely different from the world, how can God have gender? If God is male, then how can God understand problems women encounter?

The Fatherhood of God is concerned with the intimacy of God's love. When Jesus's followers asked him how to pray, he taught them to begin by saying, "Our Father" (Matthew 6:9). In the prevailing religious ethos of the day, such a practice bordered on scandalous. That is why when Episcopalians pray as Jesus taught us in the Lord's Prayer, we often introduce it with the phrase, "We are bold to say." It takes a scandalous boldness to call this almighty God our Father.

Calling God Father does not have to entail any beliefs about God's gender. God is beyond our understandings of gender. Although Jesus instructed us to call God Father, Jesus also highlighted aspects of God that seem more feminine. In this, he was continuing a trend from the Old Testament, such as when God is compared to a mother who will not forget her nursing children (Isaiah 49:15).

There comes a point where the English language fails us. In conversation about God, it is often helpful to use pronouns. But there is no pronoun in English that is beyond gender, meaning people are forced to choose between "him," "her," and "it." None of these is sufficient to talk about God.

The trouble with language and names for God reveals a basic problem in thinking about God. We can learn plenty about God from God's actions in the world. But God is also so completely different from what we know that we can never fully comprehend God. At some point, our speaking, talking, and reasoning about God reaches its limits—but God keeps going. It is a helpful reminder when thinking about theology: our knowledge about God is always limited because we are not God. It's not for nothing that Episcopalians say praying shapes believing. In prayer, we can come to deeper realizations of the loving, creative goodness of God, even if we cannot always put those realizations into precise words.

Trusting in God

The knowability or unknowability of God may mean little to a person saying the Nicene Creed in church on Sunday. Forget the finer points of God's creation; the bigger obstacle is in the first two words: "We believe." The world The Episcopal Church ministers in is marked by skepticism, cynicism, and a lack of firm commitments. To state something so clearly and firmly is to invite attention, questioning, even ridicule. "How can you believe there is a supreme God," I've been asked, "when we have seen natural disasters and disease, poverty, and illness raging out of control?" Or, "You believe in God? I believed in the tooth fairy—when I was six years old." For some people, the "We believe" begins to sound untrue. "Do I have to believe this to belong to church? What if someone finds out I'm just mumbling along or crossing my fingers behind my back?" These are real and honest concerns that make us consider what Christians mean about belief.

In English, the word **belief** has two meanings. On the one hand, belief is connected to existence. When we say of a child that she believes in the tooth fairy, we are saying the child believes the tooth fairy exists. On the other hand, belief can also be connected to trust. When I say that I believe in my friend, I'm not saying I believe my friend exists, I'm saying I trust my friend. The Latin word *credo*—the root of our English word creed—has these latter connotations. When Episcopalians say, "We believe in one God," we are expressing a belief in the existence of God. But the full force of the creed is as an expression of trust. We *trust* in one God.

Even this can be too far for some people. Why place our trust in a God who apparently allows bad things to happen to good people? Why trust a God whose existence cannot be proven? Why not just forget all about it?

God was not the only god the people of Israel knew. Indeed, at times, they worshipped some of these other gods. The early Christians also lived in a world with no shortage of other gods. At times, some Christians abandoned the worship of the God of Jesus Christ for these other deities. Few of them questioned the existence of God or gods. Rather, it was about trust. Early Christians who worshipped other gods, for instance, did not trust that they would be safe without worshipping an official Roman god.

We may not often think in these terms today, but we also live in a world with no shortage of other gods competing for our trust. Forces like money, sex, individualism, consumerism, and a whole host of others act like gods that vie for our trust. They lure us with the seductive belief that, if we only put our trust in their solutions, our problems will be solved. If only I had more money, my life would be secure. If only I could break free of this community that holds me back, I could be who I am meant to be. If only I could buy more stuff, I would feel better about myself. Through painful experience, many of us have learned that none of these gods offers the sustaining depth of goodness and love we find in the God of Jesus Christ.

To walk in the Episcopal way of following Jesus is to begin by making a basic statement of trust: we trust in this one God, who has created this good world out of love, who calls us into an intimate covenant and sends us out to make God's love known. We may not always understand God's ways. We may be tempted by other gods in our world. But we believe in a God who is worthy of our trust and who is calling us into a deeper and more full life both with God and with one another.

TO PONDER

- What words, phrases, or images help you understand God?

- What other gods in the world most frequently compete for your trust?

- In what ways have your relationships with others helped to teach you something about God? In what ways has your understanding of God taught you something about people around you?

Chapter 2

Creation, Humanity, and Sin

There is a lot of talk in Christianity about life. Jesus promised "abundant life" (John 10:10) and called himself "the way, and the truth, and the life" (John 14:6). Baptism, as we shall see, is about new life. A key Christian belief is that God is interested in offering people a new way of being. It is so central to God's love that it is part of God's very first action in the world, Creation. In **Creation**, God creates human beings to live in full and whole relationships, with God, with one another, and with the whole created world.

Genesis, the first book of the Bible, opens with two accounts of Creation. The first tells of how God created the world and all that is in it in seven days. The second focuses on the creation of the first two human beings. But both are clear that when God creates human beings, God intends to be in a special kind of relationship with them. Humans are the final act of creation, made in God's image. They are to oversee what God has created. The first man—now called Adam, in reference to the Hebrew word for "human"—names animals and tends the Garden of Eden. The special relationship God shares with Adam is marked by the fact that they walk together in the Garden of Eden and speak to one another in a way that God speaks to no other creature. Adam is naked before God, a symbol of their closeness: Adam and God have

17

nothing to hide from one another. The life that God creates for humans is marked by what we can call a **vertical relationship**—a deep relationship with God.

Relationship with God is good—but it is not enough. After creating Adam, God says, "It is not good that man should be alone; I will make him a helper as his partner" (Genesis 2:18). God creates a woman we know as Eve who becomes Adam's partner in the work God has given them. Adam and Eve are unashamedly naked in front of one another. The closeness of their relationship is summed up in the phrase the Bible uses to describe it: they became "one flesh" (Genesis 2:24). In addition to a vertical relationship, God also makes humans for a full and whole **horizontal relationship**.

The vertical and horizontal relationships in Eden share an important characteristic: they cross boundaries of difference. God is divine, and Adam and Eve are human. Adam is male and Eve is female. Yet these differences do not prevent them from being united in a single relationship. Difference is part of Creation. Indeed, in many ways, Creation is a process of differentiation. God distinguishes light from dark, earth from heaven, land from water. Our relationships are an invitation to bring together the difference of Creation into a new kind of wholeness.

Many Episcopalians read these Creation stories as revealing the kind of life God creates for God's people. It is a life marked by a particular kind of relationship: full, whole, and complete relationships both with God and with one another. The Old Testament repeatedly uses two Hebrew words to describe God's relationally focused vision for the world. The first is *shalom*, a word that means wholeness or completeness. Such wholeness comes about when the relationships that God enacted in Creation are restored. If you imagine a web of relationships running between all people and between all people and God, *shalom* describes the state of affairs when that web is unbroken.

The second word is *__hesed__*, or steadfast love. _Hesed_ is the loyalty and love of God that characterizes God's covenant relationships with

God's people. God's people are called to live that same love in their own relationships. Not only are horizontal and vertical relationships whole and complete—*shalom*—they are marked by an unwavering love—*hesed*—that is rooted in the deep, passionate commitment God makes to God's people in Creation and covenant.

Shalom and *hesed* describe an ideal state that varies from person to person and relationship to relationship. It is not God's vision that all people share a sexual relationship with one another as Adam and Eve did. Nor are we called to be so close to one another that we walk around naked. Just as there is difference in Creation, so is there difference in how *shalom* and *hesed* are embodied in relation with God and one another. But the vision of deep horizontal and vertical relationships grounded in God's love remains central.

Falling into Sin

The Creation stories in Genesis do not end with Adam and Eve dwelling in the Garden of Eden. Instead, tempted by the serpent, Adam and Eve eat from the tree of the knowledge of good and evil, though God has commanded them not to. As a result, the relationships God created begin to break down. First, Adam and Eve sew fig leaves together and hide themselves and their nakedness from God. If not broken, the vertical relationship is significantly impaired.

God surmises what has happened and confronts Adam, whose response is classic: "The woman whom you gave to be with me, she gave me fruit from the tree, and I ate" (Genesis 3:12). In other words, "She made me do it" or, "It's not my fault; you created her." Rather than being of one flesh with Eve, Adam is now pointing the finger at her, at God, at anyone but himself. The horizontal relationship that God created is now also broken. *Shalom* and *hesed* seem far away, indeed.

This is the **Fall**, the moment at which Creation departed from the ideal God had created. How did this happen? Christians have a three-letter answer: sin. Sin is central to Christian theology and to how Christians understand human nature. But those three letters can make people nervous—so nervous that many of us would rather not talk about sin at all.

The Fall, however, gives a clear picture of what sin is. **Sin** consists in turning away from God and from the fullness of life that God establishes in Creation. Sin is most clearly manifest in broken relationships, both between humans and between humans and God. As the catechism or outline of faith in the Book of Common Prayer says, "sin is the seeking of our own will instead of the will of God, thus distorting our relationship with God, with other people, and with all creation" (BCP, 848).

Often sin is so deep-seated it becomes part of the texture of our societies. Racism is one example: in it, the sin of failing to recognize the image of God in all people becomes entrenched in the structures of our society, obstructing, fraying, and terminating our relationships with one another and with God, even when we struggle to recognize it. The proof of sin is also in the breakdown of relationships we encounter in our daily lives: the death of a marriage, fissures between parent and child, or the end of a friendship. In these broken relationships we see sin at work.

It is tempting to read the story of Creation and the Fall and blame it all on Adam and Eve (or, as some Christians across the centuries have tried, only on Eve). If only they hadn't given in to temptation, if only they could have more properly seen the life God was calling them to, we never would have had the Fall. But this line of thinking misses a central point. The Creation stories are archetypes for our own lives. On some level, each of us shares with Adam and Eve the inability to resist temptation.

This is what Christians call **original sin**. "Original" in this context does not primarily mean "first." Original sin means sin is part of each one of us originally. We can't escape it. God has created us out of love, and because God has created us out of love, God allows us to make our own decisions. Christians believe each human shares the same tendency as Adam and Eve to think, "God may have said not to eat this fruit, but what harm could come of it?" As the former Archbishop of Canterbury Rowan Williams once said of original sin in a television interview, "inbuilt into human beings [is] a sort of dangerous taste for unreality."[3] Each of us has that capacity to embrace the delusion that we can find a richer or better life apart from God, that we can chart the best way forward on our own. The end result of that unreality, as we see first in the Garden of Eden, throughout Scripture and throughout human history, is the same: broken relationships, pain, and suffering.

Return to Relation

The story of the Old Testament is, in many ways, the story of God working to call God's people back to the relational ideal established in Creation. God calls a people, Israel, who are to embody in their relationships with one another *shalom* and *hesed*— wholeness and steadfast love—and to do so because of their dependence on God's love. In the **Ten Commandments** (Exodus 20:1–17; Deuteronomy 5:6–21), for instance, God outlines a society in which such relationships exist: people are not lying, murdering, or coveting; are in full relationship with their parents and neighbors; and everything is undergirded by love towards God. Generations later, God works through prophets like Isaiah, Jeremiah, Amos, and many others who make *shalom* and *hesed* the core of their message.

Both vertical and horizontal relationships are important. God's people cannot worship God without also being in right relationship with those around them. At one point, Israel's religious leaders are keen in their worship and devotion to God, making the proper observances and fasting appropriately—but they do so in

---

3. Interview on BBC *Newsnight*, 15 September 2009. Online at http://news.bbc.co.uk/1/hi/programmes/newsnight/8259172.stm.

a society in which many are neglected and ignored. God is not impressed. "Is not this the fast that I choose: to loose the bonds of injustice, to undo the thongs of the yoke, to let the oppressed go free . . . ? Is it not to share your bread with the hungry, and bring the homeless poor into your house . . . ?" (Isaiah 58:6–7).

Likewise, relationships with those around us cannot come at the expense of relationships with God. In one famous passage, the prophet Micah says, "what does the Lord require of you but to do justice, and to love kindness"—the Hebrew word for kindness here is *hesed*—"and to walk humbly with your God?" (Micah 6:8). In other words, our work for justice and *hesed* means little unless we are in right relationship with God.

If *shalom* is God's vision of relationship for the world, then sin follows closely behind. If *hesed* is how God longs for relationships to be, then fracture and division are what we add to the mix. The result is the mess that humans have routinely found themselves in, a situation that is a long way from the new life at the center of the Christian message. It is this mess that we need to be saved from. That salvation, Christians believe, is found in an itinerant religious teacher who offered a new path to the abundant life of *shalom* and *hesed*.

TO PONDER

- What words come to mind when you hear the word "sin"?

- Where do you see broken relationship in the world and in your own life?

- Where have you found glimpses of *shalom* and *hesed*?

Chapter 3

Jesus of Nazareth

Jesus of Nazareth, Jesus the Christ, my buddy Jesus, Prince of Peace, Alpha and Omega: call him what you will, but there is no escaping the fact that a Jewish teacher born more than two thousand years ago is the center of the Christian faith. Perhaps no person has had his surviving teachings dissected with such care and passion. No one's life has been as disputed, challenging, and transformative. If we want to understand what Episcopalians believe, we need to understand what Jesus is about.

Shalom and *Hesed* in Greek

Our understanding of Jesus is rooted in the first four books of the New Testament. They're called **gospels**—again, "good news"—and each is attributed to one of four evangelists: Matthew, Mark, Luke, and John. No gospel is identical to another, but each concentrates on the last few years of Jesus's life as he moved around the Holy Land, teaching, healing, and drawing crowds. In this time, he drew opposition from the religious authorities and, with the help of the ruling Roman Empire, was arrested, tried, and executed. Within days of his death, however, his followers were claiming that he had risen from the dead and continued to be with them.

We now remember Jesus as the originator of a new faith. But he understood himself to be standing in the tradition of the prophets and other witnesses to God's love who had spoken to the Jewish people in the centuries before his birth. Indeed, when Jesus was asked what was the most important thing he had to say, his answer was clear: "'You shall love the Lord your God with all your heart, and with all your soul, and with all your mind.' This is the greatest and first commandment. And a second is like it: 'You shall love your neighbor as yourself'" (Matthew 22:37–39). The teachings may sound new, but they're not. Both appear in the Old Testament (Deuteronomy 6:5 and Leviticus 19:18). Together, they are directed towards the vertical and horizontal relationships formed in Creation.

The New Testament is written in Greek, so you won't find Hebrew words like *shalom* and *hesed*. But the direction of the teaching remains the same. To love God and to love one's neighbor is to repair the broken relationships in the world and move towards wholeness, *shalom*. To do this with all one's heart, soul, and mind is the embodiment of *hesed*. The Greek word for this love is **agape**. It is the love God has for the world and the way God's people are to love one another.

God's Reign

The fruit of relationships founded on *agape* is what Jesus called the **kingdom**, or **reign**, of God. (The Gospel of Matthew calls it the kingdom of heaven.) It is the subject of Jesus's first words in his public ministry: "The time is fulfilled, and the kingdom of God has come near; repent, and believe in the good news" (Mark 1:15). In Jesus, something new is taking place.

Jesus may reference it repeatedly, but it's not always clear what the kingdom is about. It's not a political reign on earth (though many of his followers hoped it would be). It's not only a heavenly kingdom to which his followers are called after death.

Jesus's kingdom is both here and now and still to come. It is forever coming near.

One way to understand the reign of God is by the people who populate it. Jesus offers a kind of constitution of the kingdom in the **Sermon on the Mount**, one of his most famous teachings (Matthew 5–7). It is the meek, the merciful, and the persecuted who are truly blessed in this kingdom. Our commitments to one another are grounded in such truth and mutuality that we mean what we say: "Let your words be 'Yes, yes' or 'No, no'" (Matthew 5:37). The people in the kingdom are dependent on the God who has created them and loves them. Their dependence is so intimate that when they pray, the members of the kingdom do so with a familiarity and love that allows them the boldness to pray "Our Father" (Matthew 6:9). Jesus may be using different words and different images to account for his different context, but when he speaks of the kingdom he is sounding the same themes of *shalom* and *ḥesed* that are at the core of the Old Testament.

Who's In?

Who belongs to this kingdom? Episcopalians often speak of Jesus's "inclusive" ministry. Jesus deliberately sought out people from a wide range of backgrounds. In one of his first sermons, Jesus quotes the prophet Isaiah to proclaim that he has been sent "to bring good news to the poor" (Luke 4:18). Yet in the very next chapter of that gospel, he accepts an invitation to a banquet hosted by a tax collector and attended by many of the great and good in society (Luke 5:27–32). Tax collectors were many things in Jesus's time; poor was not one of them. Jesus routinely reminds his followers to pay attention to people at the periphery of society, whether that is children, beggars, or sick people. At the same time, among his followers are the wealthy and well connected. The wife of one of King Herod's senior servants follows Jesus and supports his ministry financially (Luke 8:3).

Nor did Jesus confine his attention to the Jewish people. Surprisingly, he interacted with Samaritans, a group who were related to the Jewish people but with whom they had a history of frosty, hostile relations. He teaches them, learns from them, and, famously, uses them as exemplars in some of his parables.

Inclusive, then, might not be the best word. Jesus's appeal was not to any particular group or class of people. Rather, he was interested in all people everywhere. What, then, was he up to? There are two essential truths underlying Jesus's indiscriminate attention: all people, in some way, are fallen and imperfect, yet no person is beyond the *agape* of God. Everyone is potentially included in the reign of God—but Jesus doesn't want them to stay the way they are, even if they think they've got it all figured out. Jesus's love is a transforming love.

Turn Around!

Transformation is a theme at the center of Jesus's ministry. In that opening moment, when Jesus announced the approach of the reign of God, he also called people to repent. Like sin, **repent** is a word that can make people nervous. But in the context of the story of God's love for the world, repentance is an invitation. In the midst of the broken relationships of the world, Jesus invites people to turn again to God's love and, in that love, to love one another anew. Repentance is a gift and a sign of God's love: rather than living in brokenness, Jesus is calling people to embrace whole and steadfast relationships in the kingdom of God.

But, you might ask, if we admit we were wrong, won't we be punished? This question reflects a particular understanding of justice. Do wrong, you'll be punished. Mess up, you'll really get it. The idea that each person gets what is his or her due—for good or for ill—is deeply engrained across cultures.

But Jesus rarely uses the word "justice." Instead, he talks much more about mercy and forgiveness. In one of his most famous stories, the parable of the Prodigal Son (Luke 15:11–32), a son asks his father for his inheritance early, leaves home, squanders it all, and heads back penniless. In this situation, the just thing for the father to do is reject his son or set him to work as a hired hand. Instead, Jesus tells us, the father runs out on the road and lavishly welcomes his son home before the son can even think to apologize. The father's response is not "just." But it is merciful and forgiving. It is the way God relates to God's people, if only we will turn again to God. God's love is not just, and we can only thank God that it is so.

More than a Teacher

Jesus did and said many other things. He talked about truth and freedom and how they are related. He made predictions about the age to come. He made bold assertions about his relationship with God, claiming that if people saw him, they were also looking at God. He called together a new community of followers and sent them out to share his message with others. He told stories that illustrated the reign of God. He performed miracles, giving sight to the blind, healing the sick, feeding the hungry, and making the lame walk again, demonstrating in those moments the nearness of the kingdom he preached.

Jesus's teachings are inherently appealing. Across the centuries, people have been inspired by his words about a new reign, about loving one's neighbor, about the inexhaustibility of God's love. In a divided and fractured world like our own, Jesus's teachings about a new kingdom and a transforming love have a tremendous appeal.

But Jesus's followers began to recognize something deeper in Jesus than merely a Jewish teacher. They called him the **Messiah**, a Hebrew word that means "anointed one." The Greek cognate word is **Christ**. The Messiah was the savior Israel had waited for, the one sent to redeem God's people. He would be descended from King David, the great Jewish king who reigned over a united kingdom of Israel a thousand years before Jesus's birth. For many, David's kingdom embodied what God's people continually yearned for: a peaceable, united people of God living in right relationship with God and with one another.

Jesus's ministry stirred so much energy and enthusiasm that it quickly spread beyond Galilee, his home region, and towards Jerusalem. On his arrival in the center of Jewish life, the people hailed him as the Messiah: "Hosanna to the Son of David," they cried, in words you will hear in church on Palm Sunday, the start of the holiest week in the Christian calendar. This was it. Jerusalem was under the control of the distant Roman Empire, but now the Messiah had arrived to throw off foreign rule and restore God's people and God's reign.

In Jerusalem, Jesus gathered his closest followers and shared bread and wine with them. Then, while he was praying in a garden, he was arrested, tried on trumped-up charges, and sentenced to death. The people who most vociferously called for his crucifixion were the same ones who had—just days earlier—hailed him as the Messiah. Most of his closest followers fled. Peter, one of Jesus's closest friends, was so afraid he would be associated with Jesus that he denied he even knew him. On Friday morning on a hill outside Jerusalem, Jesus was crucified. There, on the cross, he died.

To tell the story in this way, one has to wonder: why are we still talking about Jesus? His ministerial career was only a few years long. He may have said some interesting things about God and how we are to live together. But he was a failure. He didn't lead a new political empire. He couldn't even overthrow an existing one. He looks like a deluded religious teacher who bought into his own good press.

Yet not only do we still talk about Jesus today, we worship him. Christians all over the world continue to gather to break bread and drink wine as he first did. They still read the stories of his life and share them with others. They continue to believe that in his life, something of great significance took place. And that's because for Christians, Jesus's death is not the end of the story.

TO PONDER

- What aspects of Jesus's teaching do you find most appealing?

- How do you understand Jesus's call to repent, or turn around, in your own life?

- Given the people Jesus paid the most attention to during his life, where would you expect to see him in your community today?

- What is a situation in the world that you think of as unjust? Does your perspective on it change if you think in terms of mercy? How?

Chapter 4

Jesus the Christ

On the Friday that Jesus died, his followers' hopes for the future died, too. The following Sunday, the Bible tells us, two of them left Jerusalem. You can't blame them. Jerusalem had become a place of great pain for them, transformed from the site of Jesus's triumphal arrival to the place of his execution. It is a very human response to want to get as far away as possible from places and people we associate with our suffering. Jesus's followers do it. If we are honest with ourselves, we can see how we do the same.

Along the way from Jerusalem, the two followers—Cleopas and another who is not named—meet a stranger on the road to Emmaus who begins talking with them (Luke 24:13–35). Soon enough, the whole sad story of Jesus's crucifixion comes tumbling out. The stranger encourages them to look again at the stories of the Old Testament about the promised Messiah. He explains to them how, in fact, what had happened to Jesus was foretold in the Scriptures. Not surprisingly, this does little to cheer up these two travelers. Again, when you've experienced great pain and trauma, you don't want to be told, "There, there, it will be alright. You're just looking at things the wrong way." You want someone to say, "Oh, that's awful!"

As the day comes to an end, Cleopas and his friend invite the stranger to stay with them. When it comes time to eat, the stranger takes the bread, blesses it, breaks it, and gives it to them. Suddenly, they see who this stranger is: Jesus, the one on whom they had pinned their hopes. He has been resurrected from the dead and is present in their midst. Knowing it is Jesus with them, Cleopas and his friend see their encounter in an entirely new light: "Were not our hearts burning within us while he was talking to us on the road, while he was opening the scriptures to us?" (Luke 24:32). The presence of the resurrected Jesus has made them come alive in a new way. Indeed, Jesus's presence is so powerful they immediately get up from the table. Though it is by now the middle of the night, not a safe time to be traveling on the road, they set out *back* to Jerusalem. What had in the morning been a place of pain and despair from which they wanted to flee has now been redeemed. Pain and suffering have been transformed into new hope. But how?

The Story Continues

For Christians, Jesus's death on a cross is not the end of the story. His followers encountered him in risen form not only on the Emmaus road but at his empty tomb, in their room in Jerusalem, on the seashore in Galilee, and on a mountain outside Jerusalem where he ascended into heaven. These encounters helped them understand Jesus in a new way. Not only was he an itinerant religious teacher, he was the presence of God in their midst.

When people encounter the resurrected Christ, something changes in them. Cleopas and his friend went from fleeing Jerusalem to hurrying back towards it. They had not forgotten their painful memories of Jerusalem. But now they had a new way of understanding that traumatic place and even encountering it afresh. One word Christians use to describe this is **reconciliation**. The resurrected Jesus redeemed his followers' pain and guided them to a place of restoration and new hope.

Jesus does this because Jesus Christ is the Son of God, the human embodiment of God's very being. This is what Episcopalians affirm in the creed when we say Jesus is "God from God, Light from Light, true God from true God, begotten not made, of one Being with the Father." Jesus's birth is both an ordinary human birth and God's being breaking into the world. Jesus is fully human and fully God. The Council of Chalcedon, one of the councils of the early church that formed the creeds, debated this matter and concluded that Jesus Christ is "at once complete in Godhead and complete in manhood, truly God and truly man . . . of one substance with the Father as regards his Godhead, and at the same time of one substance with us as regards his manhood." This statement is so foundational, it is the first of the Historical Documents in the Book of Common Prayer (BCP, 864). What it means is Jesus is made of the same "stuff" as God; he is also made as the same "stuff" as the rest of us humans.

Still, the connection between Jesus's full humanity and full divinity and the reconciliation that takes place through his death and resurrection can be harder to see. Christians call what happened on the cross and in the empty tomb the **atonement**. But the creed never defines what happens. We simply affirm that "[f]or our sake he was crucified . . . he suffered death and was buried. On the third day he rose again." Over the centuries, Christians have offered no shortage of interpretations.

One historic interpretation, often associated with Anselm, a medieval archbishop of Canterbury, says Christ bore the sins of the world on the cross, taking on the punishment that is rightly ours. In this view, we need to be punished for our sins, but Christ intercedes and accepts it for us. A related view sees Jesus's death as a sacrifice to restore our relationship with God. Christ's death pays the debt humans owe to God. These views focus on the crucifixion. Another view, stemming primarily from the Orthodox churches of the east, shifts the emphasis to the resurrection. In returning to life, Jesus destroys death for all time, ensuring that it will never have final hold on us. Each of these views—and several others—finds echoes in the liturgies Episcopalians pray, such as when Jesus on the cross is described as a "perfect sacrifice for the whole world" (BCP, 362).

The crucifixion and resurrection can also be understood in light of the horizontal and vertical relationships God establishes in Creation and Jesus put at the center of his ministry. On the cross, Jesus embodies broken relationship. Not only have the crowds and his closest followers turned on him, he also feels abandoned by God. "My God, my God, why have you forsaken me?" he cries out (Matthew 27:46). The crucifixion is the nadir of the story of broken relationships that have characterized human society since the Fall. God takes flesh, becomes one of us, brings God's reign close to us—and even in the face of that love and mercy, we can do no other than betray, abandon, and crucify this God-made-flesh. When the love of God meets the brokenness of the world, the result is crucifixion. *Shalom* and *hesed* seem to die with Jesus.

But the *agape* of God defeats the world's brokenness. Only Jesus who is fully divine can overcome sin, and Jesus can only do so by following sin to its end point, death. Out of God's great love, God in Christ reforms broken relationships and makes us part of that new life. Christians call this **justification**, or being made right with God. Places and memories of pain are recast. Restored relationships and lives are reborn.

Now renewed and reformed, the community of followers of the resurrected Christ is sent into the world to tell others about what happened. The same world that had rejected Jesus and sent him to the cross is now invited into this community of the resurrection. In this way, the reconciliation that takes place in Christ expands even further: it knits together not only God and humans but also humans and humans. The promise of Creation and the life of Eden has been formed anew in the life, death, and resurrection of Jesus Christ. This is **salvation**. We have been saved from our death-dealing brokenness and made part of a new creation, reconciled to God and one another.

A People Far Off

If the gospel is "good news," this certainly sounds good. But it is abundantly clear that the brokenness of the world did not vanish overnight. Why not? In part, it's because people continue to run away from places and memories of pain. If we're honest about the brokenness of the world, Christians should also be honest about our part in dealing out that pain. In The Episcopal Church, when we read the stories of the crowds in Jerusalem who condemned and rejected Jesus, the congregation plays the role of the crowds. *We* shout for Jesus's crucifixion. *We* find ourselves in their midst. The crucifixion of God Incarnate shows our own brokenness and sinfulness. In some way, each of us turns away from the overwhelming love of God. It is part of who we are as human beings. This is why the world continues to be so far from the new reign that Jesus brought about in his death and resurrection.

But the first followers of Jesus are not the only ones who can encounter the resurrected Christ. Across millennia, followers of Jesus have experienced his presence in their midst. In remembering his last meal with his followers, in prayer, in action, and in worship, whole communities have had the same encounter as those followers on the road to Emmaus.

What these experiences make plain is that each of us can know the justification Jesus makes possible through his death and resurrection. The trouble is we are often unwilling to expose our brokenness and pain. We would rather cover up our failings and present our best sides to the world. This is self-justification, trying to make ourselves right with God and the world on our own. But the truth is, we will never succeed. Our sinfulness will always get in the way. The good news of the Christian faith is that God in Christ meets us in those moments, witnesses our pain, our brokenness, our flailing attempts at self-justification, and says, "I love you even here. Come live a new life." Justification is intimate and personal. It explains why the love of God, in its familiarity, honesty, and depth, in its capacity to see through our brokenness, is like no other love in the world. God's *agape* sees us in our imperfection—and loves us all the same.

If anything, the resurrected Christ is likely to show up among those who seem most alienated, like the prodigal son who squanders his inheritance and trudges back on the lonely road to his father. The Bible calls these people "far off" (Ephesians 2:13) and says that God in Christ like the father of the prodigal son comes running out to meet them and bring them near. This promise is not just for a select few. Each of us is, in some measure, far off from God's love and from love of one another. God comes to each of us—even when we do not know we need God—precisely because God loves us. God's loving approach invites us to turn around—repent—and see God's love anew.

This is what Christians call **grace**: the unearned, one-way love of God to all of God's creation. And grace, embodied in Jesus Christ, enables us to see moments of pain in new light and be reconciled to them. It enables us, as Cleopas and his friend did, to return to places of pain and see them transformed. The most authentic response to that grace is love: for ourselves, for God, for our neighbor, and for our world. Grace—*agape*—leads us into a world of *shalom* and *hesed*.

And so Jesus is not just a teacher who had some nice things to say about a new reign and the reformation of broken relationships. He is himself the way into this truth and life. His death and resurrection make it possible for sin to be overcome and this new kingdom to be present in our midst.

This is the Christian gospel, the good news of Jesus Christ. It is good, because *shalom* and *hesed* are so wonderfully good. And it is news, because there's no other place where we learn how pain is transformed, how brokenness is reconciled, and how whole communities are restored to new life.

TO PONDER

- Where have you seen brokenness and pain turned into reconciliation?

- Why do many of us find it difficult to experience the intimate love of God?

- When have you experienced being "far off" from the love of God?

Chapter 5

The Holy Spirit and the Trinity

After Jesus was killed, his followers hid out in a house in Jerusalem. Uncertain and fearful about what might happen next, they locked the doors. Would the authorities come to arrest and kill them next? Into this fear walks the resurrected Jesus. He appears in their midst and says, "Peace be with you." He breathes on them and says, "Receive the Holy Spirit." Then he sends them forth into the world (John 20:19–23).

Fifty days later, Jesus's followers are again gathered in Jerusalem. Jesus has commissioned them and sent them into the world. But he has also ascended into heaven, and they are not sure what the future holds. As they gather, the Holy Spirit sweeps among them and enables them to preach in different languages to the crowds assembled in Jerusalem (Acts 2:1–42). This is **Pentecost**, the birth day of the church. In the days and weeks after they receive the Spirit, the growing Christian community lives in a state of awe at the wonders they are now capable of doing in Jesus's name (Acts 2:43).

To meet the resurrected Jesus and live the new life he promises, followers of Jesus need the Holy Spirit, the third "person" of the three-in-one Christian God. The Holy Spirit is a gift from God through Jesus Christ, and sends people into the world to share the news of Christ's life, death, and resurrection. The Spirit transformed a religious movement in a remote corner of the Roman Empire into a church that spread across the known world.

This helps us understand the Holy Spirit's role in the early days and years of the church. But it is not always clear what role the Holy Spirit takes in the life of The Episcopal Church today. Whole Christian movements are oriented around the presence of the Holy Spirit, like the rapidly growing Pentecostal churches around the world. While charismatic revival took hold in some Episcopal churches beginning in the 1960s and many Anglicans around the world continue these practices, Christians who speak in tongues and engage in charismatic worship can seem decidedly foreign to the average Episcopal church.

In understanding the role of the Holy Spirit today, we can think back to those first disciples in Jerusalem. They experienced great fear. We've got our fears, as well: fear of losing your job, fear for your family's health, fear of any number of dramatic changes unfolding in the world. The Holy Spirit does for all Christians what the Holy Spirit did for those first followers of Jesus: the Spirit moves us from a place of fear of the future to hope at what will come. As we move to hope, we live not in fear but in wonder.

Three in One, One in Three

In the Nicene Creed, Episcopalians affirm that the Holy Spirit is "the Lord, the giver of life, who proceeds from the Father and the Son. With the Father and the Son he is worshipped and glorified." This statement leads us right into the **Trinity**, an idea that is at once at the heart of Christian theology and one of the most difficult to grasp.

Episcopalians believe God is triune—literally, three in one—a single divine entity made up of three separate persons. Over the centuries, the doctrine of the Trinity has led some people to accuse Christians of polytheism. It can stand as a major impediment to interfaith relations.

Christians have historically referred to the three persons of the Trinity as Father, Son, and Holy Spirit. We have seen in previous chapters the work and presence of both the Father and the Son throughout the history of God's dealings with God's people. (We have also seen the way these terms, despite their obvious gendered connotations in English, can point to a reality that is well beyond gender.) But the Holy Spirit can be harder to see. Christians see the Holy Spirit as the wind that blows over the waters in creation, the gift of Jesus to his followers, and the force that animates those followers throughout history. You can't picture it, but you can see what it makes possible. So the Holy Spirit is fully part of the divine being Christians worship, pervading the history of our faith because the triune God pervades that history.

Still, the Trinity poses quite a challenge since we have nothing with which to compare it. There is no human being, substance, or creation that is simultaneously three beings in one. You may be familiar with some attempts to understand the Trinity by analogy. St. Patrick used clovers in Ireland; others point to an apple, with its skin, flesh, and core wrapped into a single entity. But each of these is inherently limited and imperfect. Even when we refer to the "persons" of the Trinity, this is simply the best word that captures the individuality of each member of the Trinity. In the end, such formulations are too tidy to contain the majesty of God. The triune God will always defy full comprehension.

We can learn about the Trinity from seeing it at work. At the beginning of his ministry, Jesus is baptized in the Jordan River. As he comes out of the water, the Bible says, "the Spirit descend[s] like a dove on him" and a voice from heaven says, "You are my Son, the Beloved; with you I am well pleased" (Mark 1:10–11). Jesus is the beloved Son, over whom the Father pronounces his love, a love that the Spirit embodies. This understanding of the Father as the Lover, the Son as the Beloved, and the Holy Spirit as the Love that binds both together was articulated by an early African bishop, Augustine of Hippo, and it has been influential ever since. God's love—*agape*—is unique in the world. Where it is present, the Holy Spirit is there as well.

Jesus's baptism reveals the Trinity as a community of love. Before Creation, before people existed, God existed as a community of Father, Son, and Holy Spirit. Creation and all that follows comes as the overflowing of that community's love. The love that binds the Trinity together is an active love that is constantly engaged with the world. It is a sacrificial love that takes on death on a cross and then returns to continue to love and redeem what has been broken. The life of the Trinity embodies the relationships of *shalom* and *hesed.*

Thinking about the Trinity in this way also helps us understand what the Trinity is not. The Trinity is not one God revealed in three distinct and separate ways. Though the language of "Creator, Redeemer, and Sustainer" may be popular, Christians have historically held that such language is not adequate. It is true that God creates, redeems, and sustains. But it is not true to assert, as the language appears to suggest, that the first person of the Trinity is only a creator, that the second person only a redeemer, or that the third person has no role in creation or the first person no role in sustaining. The language of Father, Son, and Holy Spirit—despite its obvious gender-related problems—is used in Episcopal liturgies because it comes as close as we have yet figured out to capturing the fullness of the Trinity.

Intimate Participation

It is safe to say that the Trinity has been the subject of considerable theological debate throughout history. Many of the early church councils were called to sort out the details of the relationships between the persons of the Trinity. Such debates generated huge amounts of energy and vigor in the church; they also inspired fratricidal efforts to condemn and expel opponents as heretics. Such concerns can seem distant from the concerns of the world. Who cares how the persons of the Godhead relate to one another, who begot whom, and whether they are male, female, or neither? Understanding the Trinity is important. But it is taking part in the life of the Trinity that is central to the Christian life.

If the Trinity is a community of love, it is also a community of invitation. The triune God is constantly inviting all people to participate in its life of love, a participation made possible in and through Jesus Christ. In putting on flesh in the Incarnation, Christ shows us who are made of flesh how we might put on God. As Athanasius, a fourth-century bishop who was heavily involved in those early councils, wrote, "Christ assumed humanity that we might become God. . . . He endured shame from men that we might inherit immortality."[4]

Christians use the word **adoption** to describe this process. The Christian life is about being adopted into the life of the triune God. As St. Paul writes to the Romans, ". . . you have received a spirit of adoption. When we cry, 'Abba! Father!' it is that very Spirit bearing witness with our spirit that we are children of God, and if children, then heirs, heirs of God, and joint heirs with Christ" (8:15–17). The Holy Spirit adopts us into this community of love so that we come to stand in the same place as Christ in relation to God the Father.

If it sounds scandalous, it is. Standing with Christ, we hear God call us God's beloved children. This is why Christians can address God with the intimate term of Abba, or Papa. It is why Christians make the bold claim in our prayer that God is "Our Father." The Trinity is not an abstract God nor a self-contained community of three persons. Through Christ and in the power of the Holy Spirit, we participate in the life of this triune God in a real and intimate way.

In adopting us into the Trinity, the Holy Spirit repairs our broken vertical relationship with God. As we come to stand in the place of Christ in relation to the Father, what had been broken by

---

4. Athanasius of Alexandria, *On the Incarnation*, 54.

Adam and Eve in Eden is restored. And not only for Christians. All people are able to share this loving relationship with God. If that is true, then we need to relate to them in a new and different way. They, too, are God's beloved children. As we come to see others in the same light of God's love, our horizontal relationships begin to be restored as well.

Moving Past Fear

The Holy Spirit moved Jesus's first followers to new ground, teaching them there is nothing to fear in God's merciful love and nothing truly to fear in those around them. They looked toward the future with hope because they knew the Holy Spirit was drawing them into the love of God. As they heard God call them beloved, just as God calls Jesus beloved, they ventured into the world in wonder, living in awe and seeing one another as children of God.

With the Holy Spirit, fear does not have the last word. Hope and wonder do. The Christian tradition has called this state of hopeful, wonder-filled life **sanctification**. Drawn into the community of God's love, we are made holy in the light of God and understand the holiness of those we encounter as well. The work of God in the world does not end with the resurrection and ascension of Jesus Christ. The work of God continues through God's people as we are enlivened by the Holy Spirit.

The Christian faith is rooted in an invitation. A loving God invites us to participate in the new life of the resurrected Christ and share in this life through the power of the Holy Spirit. This life is marked by hope and wonder. But no matter how loving the triune God may be, no matter how strongly the Holy Spirit may urge us into the world, we are still broken and fallen. Our fears and sin have not magically disappeared. If we are to participate in this divine life, something must change. But what?

TO PONDER

- Have you ever explained the Holy Trinity to some-one, or heard it explained by someone else? What makes sense? What still mystifies you?

- How have you experienced the Holy Spirit?

- Where do you find wonder in the world?

Chapter 6

Baptism

The holiest time of each year for Christians is Holy Week, the days between Palm Sunday and Easter Sunday. In The Episcopal Church, this week is marked by a series of worship services that recall Jesus's triumphal entry into Jerusalem on Sunday, his last meal with his followers on Thursday, and his arrest and crucifixion on Friday. By Saturday, the day after Jesus's death, the world is in turmoil. God's Son has been made human and we have put him to death. What hope is there for the world? What hope is there for us?

As the sun sets on Saturday, Episcopalians gather by dim candlelight. It is the darkness of night and the gloom of sin. From the earliest days of the church, Christian communities have gathered at this time for what we now call the **Great Vigil of Easter**. The people process into the church with the first light of Easter, a single candle representing the undying love of God. In the semi-darkness, the congregation hears the story of God's loving, saving action in history. From the moment of creation, when God spoke into being a world in which relationships were whole and strong, to the covenants God made with Noah, Abraham and Sarah, and many others, to God's salvation of the Israelites in the waters of the Red Sea, and God's presence with God's people in Israel, God's love for the world has remained steadfast.

But the church remains in shadow. Though God acts out of love for the world, Jesus is still in the grave. God loved the world so much that God sent God's son—and the world put him to death. Even as we remember the love of God, in this liturgy we also remember our complicity in the broken relationships of the world and our deep yearning for transformation and new life.

Then comes the moment when it all changes. Having heard these stories, having heard of God's love, the priest asks the congregation if they would like to walk in a new way. What could this path be? For millennia, the liturgy has provided the same answer: baptism.

From Death to Life

If you belong to an Episcopal church or have attended one enough times, chances are you have seen or participated in a baptism. One of the preferred occasions is the Easter Vigil, when we walk in the footsteps of those early **catechumens** (or candidates who undergo formation for baptism). Baptisms can also happen at other times of the year. Shortly after the sermon on a Sunday morning, the priest might gather with a baby and her family around the font, a basin that holds water. The priest prays over the water, the family and members of the congregation make promises, and then the priest gently pours water over the baby's head. She has been baptized, washed fresh and clean. The details can vary. Sometimes adults are baptized. Other times the baptism happens outside, in a lake or a river or an ocean. Sometimes the person is dunked fully under water and other times only a few drops fall on the person's head.

However it is done, the meaning of baptism remains the same, and it is the meaning revealed in the Easter Vigil. At its core, baptism is about death and new life. Christians descend into the water and join Christ in his death. It is fitting, since water is not exactly safe; you can drown in it. In baptism, we succumb to the waters, dying to our sin and brokenness.

Immediately after the baptisms at the Easter Vigil, the congregation proclaims the central truth of the Christian faith: "Alleluia, Christ is risen!" Just as Christ rose from the dead, so we rise from the drowning of baptism. Water is also the stuff of life. As we rise from the water, we are also raised to new life with Christ. As St. Paul wrote to the Romans: "Do you not know that all of us who have been baptized into Christ Jesus were baptized into his death? Therefore we have been buried with him by baptism into death, so that, just as Christ was raised from the dead by the glory of the Father, so we too might walk in newness of life" (Romans 6:3–4).

It is a startling thing, in this day and age, to say that we are baptized into death. Our world is achievement-oriented. I've experienced this in school and in work, of course, with the pressure to produce more and perform better. I've experienced it in family life, like the constant pressure to do everything "right" for your children—to throw the best birthday parties, take the most interesting vacations, get them into the right schools. Parents of every background hope our children will land on paths of achievement and success as early as they can. Baptism offers none of this. Instead, it invites us to surrender to God's love and follow Jesus, who, by the standards of the world, was a failure.

But it is through baptism, Christians claim, that change happens in the world and happens in us. As we do the same thing Jesus did—dying and rising again—we become new people incorporated into the new life offered by the risen Christ. We can die to our society's focus on achievement and instead be adopted by the Holy Spirit into the Trinitarian life of *agape*. We hear God call us God's beloved child. In baptism, Christians believe, we become so closely linked with Christ that we become part of his resurrected body.

Early Christian communities would stay up all night reading the stories of God's love for the world. They would wait until dawn—the hour of Jesus's resurrection and the approach of new light—before baptizing the newest members of the community and welcoming them into the community of resurrected life. Most Episcopal Easter Vigils are over well before dawn, but the meaning remains the same. Change needs to happen in the world. Through baptism, that change begins in us.

The Baptismal Life

Baptism is a **sacrament**, "the outward and visible sign of an inward and spiritual grace" (BCP, 857). The water is the outward sign of the inward grace of union with God, brought about through Christ's death and resurrection. Through this sacrament, we are incorporated into the new life of his risen body. We are not the same as we were before.

But here you may want to pause. "I am baptized," you might be thinking, "and there are plenty of days when I don't exactly live like Christ's new life is in my own." That is certainly true in my own life. Or, you might know someone else who is baptized and notice, perhaps, that they have not sufficiently died to the old life of sin. There's no escaping this. The sacraments are not magic. The waters of baptism do not immediately transform us into perfect Christ-like beings who embody *shalom* and *ḥesed* in all we do.

Baptism sets an orientation for our life. On the one hand, baptism frankly acknowledges our imperfection. Why would we have to die to ourselves and to our sins if we were not broken? At the same time, baptism also recognizes the new life that is now possible in the risen Christ. The life of a baptized person—the life of a Christian—is about staying aware of both the death and the new life in our daily journeys and moving more fully towards the latter. Some Episcopal churches put little basins of water near their entrances so that people may make the sign of the cross on themselves with the water as they enter the church. This practice reminds us of our baptism (the water), our sinfulness (the cross), and how we continually seek to live a new life. Some days, my own brokenness and the brokenness of the world weigh me down. Other days, I feel gloriously and newly alive in Christ's resurrected life. Like many Episcopalians, I was baptized as an infant, a practice not shared by all Christians. There are many reasons to baptize infants but one thing about it is sure: it gives us a whole lifetime to figure out how to walk in the new life that is made known in Christ.

A Covenantal Life

Baptism makes sense only in light of Christ's death and resurrection. But it also points us back to Jesus's own baptism (Mark 1:10–11). That happened not at the end of his ministry but at the beginning. It is only after his baptism that Jesus begins to preach, teach, and call people to turn again to God's love. The same is true for each baptized person. If our society orients us towards achievement, baptism orients our lives in ways that send us out into the world.

In The Episcopal Church, we find the outlines of that orientation in the **Baptismal Covenant**, a set of questions and answers in the baptismal service (BCP, 304–5). The Covenant begins by calling those who are to be baptized and the entire congregation to affirm their faith in the triune God, who draws us into a community of *agape*. Then the Covenant invites people to continue in the teaching of the church and in the celebration of the sacraments; to reaffirm our commitment to repentance and renewal and the centrality of telling others about the good news of Jesus Christ; and to commit ourselves to service in the world, working towards a day when God's wholeness will be known in the lives of every person and across the earth. This is the outline of baptismal living.

The covenant is a tall order. As we make these vows, we know we will continue to fall short. But we make the promises just the same, because they are an expression of the direction we want to see our lives and the lives of those around us move. We want to see lives marked by—and this will come as no surprise—full and steadfast relationships, both between ourselves and God and between ourselves and all other people and all of creation.

This covenant only makes sense in light of what Christ has done in dying and rising again. Because of all that he overcame, we move forward with confidence knowing that in baptism we are adopted as God's children and called God's beloved. Sin and brokenness are not the end. Christ is risen, and through baptism we can join in the new life he promised.

I am intentional in the use of "we" language. There is always a danger that the Christian faith appears individualistic: "The Holy Spirit adopts *me* into the life of the Trinity." "In baptism, *I* die and rise again with Christ." In reality, as we are incorporated into Christ's body in baptism, we are also incorporated into a life with all others in that body, past, present, and future. Baptism links us to all other followers of the resurrected Christ. And that leads us to the church.

TO PONDER

- What areas of your life do you wish you could live differently? In other words, what do you seek to "die" to? In which areas do you wish you were more fully alive?

- In what ways does the Christian faith challenge our achievement-focused society?

- Have a look at the Baptismal Covenant on pages 304–305 of the Book of Common Prayer or at www.bcponline.org. Which parts most resonate for you?

Chapter 7

Church

At the center of his teaching, Jesus put the kingdom of God, an expansive, transforming reign. But the kingdom isn't the primary carrier of Jesus's life and message in the world today. That role falls to something much more mundane: the church.

Jesus himself barely used the word "church." It appears only a handful of times in the gospels. If you are interested in living the new life of Jesus, you could be forgiven for thinking the church is something you can do without.

The actions of the church, both in history and in our own time, make some people want to disregard the institution even more. Church leaders and institutions launched the Crusades, became allies and defenders of repressive regimes, and repeatedly stood (and stand) in the way of social progress. In our own time, the church can be as much a cause for disappointment as it can for inspiration or enthusiasm. For younger generations, church may just be the strange building on the corner that tells you who you can—but mostly cannot—have sex with.

Yet seeing the church this way misses a crucial point: the church is an integral part of the good news of Jesus Christ. Early on, people trying to follow the way of Jesus realized that they had to reckon with the church. The Acts of the Apostles tells us the

extraordinary ways that Jesus's first followers began to develop
the church in the power of the Spirit. Church life is a key concern
of the apostle Paul and other authors in the New Testament. To
be a Christian is to be a member of the church. Strange as it may
sound to modern ears, that claim is deeply good news.

A Single Body

Baptism makes us part of Christ's risen body. It adopts us into a
new relationship with God and with all the rest of the baptized,
who are equally beloved of God. This explains the key New Testament idea that it is impossible to follow God in Christ on your
own. We actually need other people if we want to know the fullness of God's *shalom* and *ḥesed*.

St. Paul offers one of his longest teachings on what it means
to be part of **Christ's body** in his first letter to the Corinthians
(11:17—12:31). It turns out that when the Corinthians come together to remember the Last Supper, they are divided. Rather
than eating together, they divide themselves according to class.
The rich eat well, while the poor eat separately and eat not much
at all.

This horrifies Paul. The Christian community should not be
reproducing the divisions of the world. Instead, Paul explains, the
Christian community should transcend these divisions. He goes
on to compare the community to a body. Each part of the body
needs the others to function. If the whole body were an eye, how
could it smell? If it were all nose, how could it hear? Similarly
for the followers of Jesus, each person has gifts to offer the whole
community, and no person has everything she needs to follow Jesus on her own.

This is why membership in the body of Christ is such good
news. If we want to be led more deeply into the way of Jesus,
we need other people. There are people who need us so they can
do the same. The Christian community is one where people are

constantly giving to others. It is equally—though this is easy to forget—a community where all are continually receiving from one another.

You may have been taught when you were growing up not to talk to strangers. That may be good advice for a child, but it is awful advice for a Christian. There are people we do not know, people we have not yet met, people we need to enrich our lives of faith (and who need us to enrich theirs). No doubt, they'll be different from us. In the same way that the horizontal and vertical relationships in the Garden of Eden crossed lines of difference, the body of Christ brings together all kinds of difference—gifts, backgrounds, ways of following God—into a single whole.

Who Belongs?

Still, the body of Christ could seem like just another club. Clubs have presidents, treasurers, secretaries, and so forth, with each person performing her own role. The church does too. But one aspect of the body of Christ distinguishes it from other organizations: we do not get to choose who else belongs; God does. The body of Christ is formed by baptism, and people are led to baptism in response to God's love. It is not for us to say that they cannot belong or, worse yet, that we do not want them to belong. God has joined us together in one body from different backgrounds and called us to give to and receive from one another. That is the gift of baptism. One of the saddest and most painful moments for Christians is when a church community splits and divides. A divided Christian community is a community that will be unable to fully follow Jesus. It lacks the gifts necessary to do so.

Membership in the body of Christ goes against the grain of everything contemporary western societies teach us. In most cases, if we don't like something or don't like a group, we can get up and leave. Or we can organize to boot the offending member out. Our political parties, for instance, have become very good at purifying themselves and basing themselves on an ever narrower set of interests. It is an example of the way communities tend toward division and fracture. The church, by contrast, tends toward wholeness. In church we may often encounter other Christians who seem so different we want to scream in frustration, "I have no need of you!" For Paul that is precisely what one part of the body cannot say to another. Instead, these moments of frustration and anger become opportunities for prayer and a deeper living into our Baptismal Covenant, as we discern just what it is we have to both give to and receive from these other members.

What this makes clear is that the body of people who follow Jesus is a **counter-cultural community**. Jesus himself tells his followers that they are not of this world (John 17:14). Paul makes the claim explicit when he tells Christians in Rome not to be conformed to this world but to be transformed by the renewing of their minds. Only then will they be able to discern the will of God (Romans 12:2). We express our non-conformity to the world through our relationships within the Christian community. Nowhere else in the world do we put such emphasis on both giving and receiving from one another, on forgiveness and reconciliation, on *shalom* and *hesed*. Christian relationships embody—in whatever imperfect way—the wholeness of life that God promises and re-creates through Christ.

Community of Reconciliation

It is easy to idealize the Christian community. As anyone in or near a church must know, the reality of church life is often division and conflict. That this division can frequently seem petty and small-minded only makes the contrast between vision and reality worse.

Jesus addresses this situation in one of the rare instances when he uses the word "church." "If another member of the church sins against you," he begins, "go and point out the fault when the two of you are alone" (Matthew 18:15). Conflict happens in the church. That does not surprise Jesus and it should not surprise us. Followers of Jesus are called to work to repair the breach. The same reconciliation that God wrought through Christ in the world becomes the work of Christians in the church.

Jesus is specific about how to go about this repair: if the person does not listen when you visit him or her, go back with one or two other people; if that fails, bring it up publicly in the church; if that does not work, "let such a one be to you as a Gentile and a tax collector" (Matthew 18:17). Before you assume this means write them off, remember Jesus's openness to Gentiles and tax collectors—a tax collector, Matthew, was remembered as the author of this gospel. What is clear is that broken relationships need to be mended, and Jesus sends Christians to continue this work even when it seems extreme. Jesus concludes the teaching with one of his better-known teachings: "For where two or three are gathered in my name, I am there among them" (Matthew 18:20). When members of the church are working toward reconciliation, Jesus is present in their midst.

Jesus's teaching defines the church. We are a community of reconciliation. This is not to say we are a community of people who are fully at peace and perfectly embody *shalom* and *hesed*. Rather, the church is the community of people who understand the importance of living in relationship with all those whom God has called into the body of Christ. We honestly acknowledge that this pattern of living will lead to conflict, and we do not respond by walking away from the church or from those members with whom we are in conflict. Rather, we understand that we are the community of people who by God's grace continue to work toward the reconciliation that is God's vision for the world.

The church believes so strongly in this vision of a reconciled community that we cannot keep the message to ourselves. In the same way that the first followers of Jesus Christ were sent into the world by him empowered by the Holy Spirit, members of the

Christian community are called, each in our own way, to take this message further and wider into the world, so that the body of Christ and reign of God may continue to expand.

One, Holy, Catholic, and Apostolic

In its constitution, The Episcopal Church defines itself as part of the "one, holy, catholic, and apostolic church." The phrase comes from the Nicene Creed. Those words are small, but they carry great weight:

- The church is **one** because it is the one body of Christ into whom all are called.
- The church is **holy** because it is a distinctive and counter-cultural community that seeks to live as vessels for God's blessing in the world. The holiness that God calls God's people to has always been a holiness that sets it apart from the world around it.
- The church is **catholic** because it is, in the literal meaning of the word, universal. Not only does it cover the world but it teaches all people everything they need to know for wholeness in life, namely the reconciliation with God and one another that comes through Christ.
- And the church is **apostolic** because, like the first followers of Jesus, it witnesses to the resurrection and is sent into the world.

When we remember that the word "believe" in the Nicene Creed also means "trust," it is right to be astonished by the affirmation in the creed: we trust in this one, holy, catholic, and apostolic church. Each of us has had experiences of church that hurt and disappoint us and leave us a long way from *shalom* and _hesed_. To the extent that the church is involved in causing pain, in breaking relationships and re-creating the Fall, it is an indictment of the church, laying bare its own brokenness and imperfection.

The church can never be the kingdom of God, but it does offer a sign of this reign. Christians continue to place our trust in the church because at the core of its life is a practice that offers us a glimpse of this kingdom and directs us in the ways of *shalom* and *hesed*.

TO PONDER

- When is a time you have found the church to be "holy," that is, truly distinct and reflecting the life of God into the world around it? In what ways can the church offer a counter-cultural model to the society we live in?

- Have you ever struggled with someone in the body of Christ? How did you deal with that conflict? Did it lead you into a deeper relationship with God and other Christians, or further away?

Chapter 8

Eucharist

On the night before he died, Jesus gathered his closest followers around him and shared a meal with them. It was a simple meal, some bread and wine, the basic foodstuffs that the followers of this wandering teacher might eat each night. As he took the bread, Jesus gave thanks, broke it, and told them to eat it "in remembrance of" him. As he took the wine, he also blessed it and called it his own blood. It would soon be poured out, he said, and his followers should drink "in remembrance of" him (Matthew 26:26–29; Luke 22:14–20; 1 Corinthians 11:23–26).

That command—to eat bread and drink wine in remembrance of Christ—may be the command that has been obeyed by more people in a greater variety of circumstances across generations and centuries than any other. Early Christians hiding from Roman authorities ate and drank in remembrance of Christ. Kings and queens did so before heading out to battle. Oppressed and suffering laborers have found new strength in the bread and wine of Jesus.

For Episcopalians, this meal is the center of our religious practice. We call it the **Eucharist**, a Greek word that means "thanksgiving." In the last generation—since the 1979 revision of the Book of Common Prayer—the Eucharist has become the principal Sunday morning service in Episcopal churches. If it is true that our praying shapes our believing, and that you'll know what we believe by how we pray, then it is wise to watch the Eucharist closely.

The Shape of the Liturgy

Walk into an Episcopal service, and you will almost certainly see a priest standing in front of the congregation taking wine and wafers (every now and then, it is real bread), praying over them, and offering them to God and God's people. The priest could be clothed in elaborate vestments and surrounded by clouds of incense, singing the entire prayer. Or the priest could be in sandals and shorts with a simple stole around her neck. Either way—and many ways in between—is a holy and true way of following Jesus's commandment at the Last Supper.

Jesus had a varied ministry and did much more than eat with his close friends. Why do we focus on this meal? The answer lies in the *shalom* and *hesed* at the root of God's love for the world. The Eucharist reminds us, recalls for us, and incorporates us into God's loving plan for the restoration and wholeness of the world.

Think about a Eucharistic service you've recently attended in an Episcopal church. Chances are it included a number of features, like reading and reflecting on the Bible and praying for the world, the church, and those in need. Each element is important, but this chapter will consider four: members of the congregation confess and are absolved of their sins, pass the peace, offer gifts at the altar, and receive the bread and wine. Each of these actions points us towards God's wholeness and steadfast love.

Confession

At some point in a Eucharistic service, members are invited to **confess** their shortcomings and failings. This is a time for frank honesty with God. "By what we have done, and by what we have left undone" (BCP, 360), we have been unable to live God's love in our own lives and with others. We have not loved God whole-heartedly, nor have we loved our neighbors as we have loved ourselves. Without fear or shame, we are admitting sin is part of human existence and part of us. In confession, we are offered and reminded of God's loving invitation to repentance, to turn again to God's steadfast love and know God's mercy and forgiveness. When the priest absolves the congregation and tells them to be "strengthen[ed] in all goodness" (BCP, 360), the vertical relationship that was broken in Eden is restored.

Peace

Following confession, the priest announces Christ's **peace** to the congregation. In some congregations, this can be a full-on experience. People shake hands or hug one another and say something like, "Peace be with you." Sometimes it lasts a few moments, and other times it feels more like a seventh-inning stretch in a baseball game. But it's a practice with deep roots in the Bible. In fact, instead of handshakes and hugs, Paul told Christians they should greet one another with a holy kiss (Romans 16:16). Handshaking is the Episcopal version of that kiss.

The true meaning of this moment comes from the Sermon on the Mount. Jesus taught that "when you are offering your gift at the altar, if you remember that your brother or sister has something against you, leave your gift there before the altar and go; first be reconciled to your brother or sister, and then come and offer your gift" (Matthew 5:23–24). We cannot rightly worship God without sharing full and whole relationships with other followers of the God we know in Jesus Christ. In passing the peace, the horizontal relationship that was broken in Eden is also restored.

This can sound strange in the context of our actual worship. It is not as if the single moment of confession and absolution suddenly perfects us into sinless beings. But these moments serve as prompts for prayer and action. When you pass the peace, for instance, ask yourself: With whom in this group of people am I trying to avoid shaking hands? Does it feel particularly false with anyone when I say to them, "Peace be with you"? Beyond the people present in the congregation, the peace prompts further reflection. Who is not in this congregation? With whom am I missing opportunities for reconciliation because of their absence from this Eucharistic community? To take one example, many Episcopal churches remain functionally segregated along racial lines. Yet we know how urgently the United States needs racial reconciliation. During the peace we come face-to-face with the ongoing need for reconciliation and the importance of continually enlarging our Eucharistic communities by addressing the deep reasons why we remain so separate.

Offering

Following the confession and the peace, Episcopalians **offer** our gifts before the altar. For most people, this means writing a check or electronically uploading a donation for the work of the church, though in some congregations it includes giving physical, tangible objects for ministry. At a congregation where I once worshipped in South Sudan, a woman brought forward several bundles of corn on her head. It was what she had to give for the work of the church. Regardless of the form, when the gifts of money, bread, wine, and more are placed on the altar, we are reminded that we cannot celebrate the Eucharist alone. Not only do we rely on the goodness of God, who has provided all things and to whom we merely return the gift, but we also rely on one another. On our own, we cannot follow Jesus or even begin to embody God's reign. But with the gifts of others and our own, all offered before God, we can.

Eucharistic Prayer

Only after all this is complete does the priest begin the **Eucharistic Prayer** over these gifts. In this prayer, the priest remembers all that God has done for us in and through Jesus Christ. The Eucharist constantly reminds us—and yes, we frequently forget—of the love of Christ, the forgiveness of sins, and the invitation to new life that we receive in his life, death, and resurrection. The priest then remembers the specific events of Jesus's final meal with his followers: the taking, the blessing, the breaking, and the giving of bread and wine. She invokes the Holy Spirit over the bread and wine so that Christ comes to be truly, wondrously present in them and in us.

The Kingdom in Our Midst

Confession, peace, offering, Eucharist—these parts of the liturgy and many others work together for a unified whole. That whole is not simply a memorial of Jesus's last meal with his followers. It is the breaking into the world of the kingdom of God, the realization of God's plan for the world. In these Eucharistic moments, the people of God are at peace with one another and at peace with God. *Shalom* and *ḥesed* are realized. Reconciliation is at hand. Episcopalians sometimes call Eucharist **Communion**, invoking a biblical word that refers to our oneness before God. If we could, we would hold onto this moment forever.

Of course we cannot. We may have been absolved of our sins—but we are still imperfect and broken people. We may have passed the peace—but our communities are still fraught with conflict. We may have offered our gifts—but we still struggle to give and receive from one another. The Eucharist can be described in lofty, transcendent terms, but most people's experience is much more banal: the priest loses his place on the page, an acolyte distractedly picks her nose, a father shushes his son, a teenager looks out the window in boredom. This is it? This is what Christians are all about?

This contrast reveals one of the most difficult ideas in Christian theology. In the Eucharist, two things are simultaneously true: First, we are already actually part of a community of *shalom* and _hesed_. Second, we are still living apart from God's plan for the world. In the confession and peace, for instance, we are not only reminding ourselves of the importance of true and right relationships with one another and with God, we are also actually experiencing them in those very moments. A word to describe the Eucharist, then, is **proleptic**: we are already in the kingdom and we are not yet there.

The already/not-yet nature of the Eucharist is summed up in what happens after the priest prays over the bread and wine: she breaks the bread, the body of Christ. "Christ our Passover is sacrificed for us," she says. In Christ's death and resurrection, we are incorporated into a community of _shalom_ and _hesed_, the body of Christ. Equally, however, like the bread broken and held up for all to see, that body of Christ is a broken body, a brokenness we see in the fracture and division in our lives and in the world.

In that moment of both incorporation and brokenness, we pray the prayer that Jesus taught us, the Lord's Prayer. We pray for God's kingdom to come, even as we experience it in the Eucharistic meal. We ask for forgiveness and the grace to forgive others, even as we experience both in the worship. We pray for deliverance, even as we know God's grace and deliverance moving through our being.

Then and only then do we receive the bread and wine, the body and blood of Christ. The verb is important here. We do not "get" or "take" Eucharist. We receive it as the gift of God's great love that it is.

Thanksgiving for New Life

Like baptism, Eucharist finds its true expression in the Easter Vigil service held the Saturday night before Jesus's resurrection. After baptizing new Christians into the new life of Christ at the Vigil, the community celebrates the Eucharist. It is so very right to celebrate the Eucharist in the first light of Easter morning, because the Eucharist makes sense only in the light of Christ's resurrection. It is only because of the resurrection that we have confidence that the deadly forces of the world have been overcome and that we can live like the redeemed children of God that we already are.

The sequential order of the Easter Vigil is important: by first dying and rising with Christ in baptism, we are then incorporated into his Eucharistic life. The Easter Vigil is the clearest explanation why The Episcopal Church, in common with many other churches, teaches that baptism is to precede Eucharist. The latter makes little sense without the former.

The church, it has been said time and again, is never more truly the church than when it is celebrating the Eucharist. In the Eucharist, we realize the church's identity as the community of *shalom* and _hesed_ that God desires to see throughout the world. In the Eucharist, we are truly the reconciled people of God, at peace with God and with one another.

Then the liturgy of the Eucharist ends. But it ends with significant words: "Go in peace to love and serve the Lord." The Eucharistic people are sent, sent to take the Eucharist into the world.

TO PONDER

- What non-monetary offerings could you make for the work of the church?

- In what moments of the Eucharist have you felt particularly close to God and the other members of the congregation?

- What has been your experience of the relationship between baptism and Eucharist? How similar or different is it to what is described in this chapter?

Chapter 9

Mission

Some years ago, I signed up to work for The Episcopal Church as a missionary in South Africa. But before I signed on, I hesitated over the very word "missionary." It is a word—along with "evangelist"—that for many people has particular associations. You may picture a white man preaching the gospel to the native people of Africa, a revivalist tent preacher making his way from camp to camp across the country, or a person handing out slips of paper with Bible verses in front of the mall. These stereotyped images had a powerful hold on my imagination. I was not initially sure I wanted to associate myself with this history.

Mission and evangelism are complicated theological terms with mixed histories. In the long history of Christian mission, some Christian **missionaries** have challenged injustice, stood up for the oppressed, and served as icons of the kingdom of God. Other missionaries have colluded with agents of power, preached particular cultural practices rather than the transcendent gospel of Jesus Christ, and generally failed to embody Christ's transforming love. This makes some Christians shy away from the word mission altogether.

But even a cursory survey of twenty-first-century culture shows there is no shortage of missionaries carrying messages forth. They're just not missionaries for the good news of Jesus Christ. Look at the revival-esque fervor surrounding TED talks as they go viral on the Internet and promise technical solutions to life's problems. Look at how the forces of commerce have turned Christian holy days like Christmas and Easter into feasts to the great god of consumerism.

If Christians will not be missionaries and share the good news, there are plenty of other people and forces eager to fill that vacuum.

Church Dismissed

At its root, the word "**mission**" means "sent." Christians are people who are sent into the world. Throughout his ministry, Jesus was constantly sending his followers into the world to share his message and his ministry. After his resurrection, Jesus told his followers that, as he had been sent into the world by God the Father, so he was sending them into the world in the power of the Holy Spirit. They were to go to all the nations, making disciples, teaching others about Jesus, and leading them to membership in the body of Christ through baptism (John 20:21–22; Matthew 28:19–20).

The Episcopal prayer book defines mission as "restor[ing] all people to unity with God and each other in Christ" (BCP, 855). It is a short statement that encompasses all that we have seen in this book. The unity of relationship that God created in Eden was sundered by the Fall. In Christ, these relationships are reformed. As his followers, our mission is to share that good news so that both our horizontal and vertical relationships may be restored in and through Christ.

Paul uses another word to describe a similar idea: **reconciliation**. Through Christ, he writes, we have been reconciled to God. That reconciliation is not the end of the story, however. Instead, we are given that same ministry of reconciliation to share with the world (2 Corinthians 5:18–19).

Our sending into the world as ministers of reconciliation is linked with the final act of the Eucharist. Having made peace with one another and with God, and having been reconciled to the reign of God in the Eucharist, Episcopalians are told to "Go." This is the **dismissal**, a word that literally means "sending away." There is a clear and close connection between Eucharist and mission. The reconciliation and unity of relationship that is the purpose of mission is found in the Eucharist. Christians can't help but want to take the Eucharist into the world to draw more people into this community of people who have died and been raised again with Christ and live his *shalom* and *ḥesed*. At its core, mission is the expansion of the Eucharistic community through baptism.

Sharing Good News

The good news Christians have to offer is, at its core, the Eucharist. But what about the competing messages in the world. They sound awfully good. What makes the Christian message different?

One difference is the way in which we communicate it. The good news of Jesus Christ is ultimately about the relationships we share with God, one another, and the world. So it takes a community of people to share the Christian message. Jesus told his followers as much: "By this everyone will know that you are my disciples," he told them, "if you have love for one another" (John 13:35). Relationships of reconciled love within the Christian community can teach other people more about Jesus than a slew of words ever could.

In one of the earliest stories of the Christian community after Pentecost, the link between community and mission is particularly clear. "All who believed were together and had all things in common; they would sell their possessions and goods and distribute the proceeds to all, as any had need" (Acts 2:44–45). This describes the life of reconciled relationships and restored community in Christ. That life had a clear evangelical impact: "Day by day the Lord added to their number those who were being saved" (Acts 2:47).

If mission is about reconciliation, the life of the community in mission must exemplify this restoration of relationship. That means mission is for all Christians, not a small subset we set apart. The church in mission is a whole community of difference, with each person giving and receiving gifts to one another. That community offers a model of life that is holy and abundant, and which the world can find no place else. Jesus summarizes this vision in a prayer for his followers shortly before he is arrested. He prays that "they may all be one . . . so that the world may believe" (John 17:21). Our life of reconciled diversity—our unity—is central to our witness about the good news of Jesus Christ. In order to be Christians in mission, we need other Christians, even and especially those who seem most different from us.

This can seem like an impossible dream. Not only are Christians dismissed and called to take the Eucharist into the world, but we have to do it with other Christians who can drive us absolutely crazy with their different beliefs, challenging personalities, and odd practices. It's enough to make you despair of the entire task and simply give up, ignore the dismissal, and stay in your safe, familiar church community. And it's true: there is a constant temptation to make mission safe by making it less about Jesus Christ and more about ourselves and our church. "Here's what I really like about our community," we might say. "I think you'll like it, too." Our efforts toward mission look more like getting people to join our church club than about sharing the good news of the new life promised in Christ's death and resurrection. Mission is not primarily about church, however; it's about Jesus.

Eucharistic Spirituality

God's call to mission and evangelism can seem burdensome in a context where fewer people come to church and even fewer seem to think it matters. Soon, our fear of the future and of the cultures emerging around us takes over, and we lose sight of the hope and wonder toward which the Holy Spirit calls us.

We can approach mission by asking this question: if mission is expanding the Eucharist, how can we begin taking portions of the Eucharist into the world? For instance, we read the Bible in the Eucharist. We can also read the Bible in the world. What if you read the story about Jesus feeding the thousands in front of a food bank or a homeless shelter?

We acknowledge our shortcomings and failings in the church. We can also confess our sins in the world. Our economy is structured such that we can hardly avoid shopping at businesses that treat workers poorly or source products in ways that are damaging to the environment. These purchases embody the brokenness that exists in our world and in ourselves. Even as we proclaim *shalom* and _hesed_, we participate in a world that actively works against this wholeness. So what happens if we offer confession each time we shop at such a business, eat a meal whose preparation hurts the earth or other humans, or fill our gas tank? It is a first step in amending our ways to align our choices and witness with the reign of God.

In the Eucharist, we make peace with one another. Eucharistic mission invites us to put ourselves in new positions so that we can seek reconciliation with those who are not in our churches on Sunday but are equally God's children.

These are just a handful of examples, and mission takes as many different forms as there are Christians. But the idea remains the same: the Eucharistic liturgy needs to be freed from the church building and taken into the world. As we do so, we become missionaries of Christ's good news.

Such an approach to the world requires a particular disposition, the same one Jesus modeled throughout his ministry.

- Jesus was **open** to those around him, welcoming children, women, and the sick whom others sought to exclude.

- Jesus chose to be **vulnerable**, a vulnerability made most clear on the cross.
- Jesus was **receptive**, willing to encounter, listen to, and engage those who were different from him and to see where those new relationships led.
- Jesus was **humble**, at once confident of his position before God but refusing to insist on special treatment or to make himself the center of attention.
- Jesus was **fearless**. It's not that he did not have fear— we don't know if he did—but he did not let this fear control him.
- Jesus trusted—or was **faithful** to—what God had set before him.

These attributes—openness, vulnerability, receptivity, humility, fearlessness, faithfulness—are some of the hallmarks of what we might call a spirituality of mission, the sort of approach that Christians can take to the world. Practices like these allow us to approach our sisters and brothers in Christ and ask how we may *together* take the Eucharist into the world. Characteristics like these allow us to approach all of God's children and welcome them into the reconciled community of the Eucharist.

Developing such a spirituality is not something we do on our own. It is only by coming to dwell in the risen Christ, and to know God's call on us as God's beloved, that we are enabled to go forth into the world. And so we return to the Eucharistic community to be reconciled again to God and one another, and to see the kingdom of God arrayed in our midst. And then we are dismissed and sent forth again to continue to draw more people into that community of God's love.

If we place our trust in the Christian gospel, then mission is the natural result. The good news of Jesus Christ is so powerful and wonderful that there is no reason why we would not want to share it, especially in communities where it is quickly disappearing.

TO PONDER

- What do you associate with the words "missionary" and "evangelist"?

- In what ways can your community take the Eucharist into the world? In what ways can your community listen to what is already present in the communities around you?

- What obstacles prevent you from taking the good news into the world?

Chapter 10

The End

The Nicene Creed—as well as this book about theology—ends with, well, the end. Christian faith is oriented towards what will happen in the future. Jesus himself devoted a considerable amount of his time to telling his disciples about what was yet to come. In some of his letters, Paul was convinced the end was coming soon. We call these passages "**apocalyptic**," a word that means "revealing." They unveil something of what will happen at the end of Creation.

The theological word for this is **eschatology** from the Greek word for end. End has a double meaning: conclusion, as well as ultimate purpose. It is an area of theology that some Christians, including many Episcopalians, would be happy to ignore. It is much easier to understand how Christian faith is rooted in the past (the creating, loving, and saving action of God) or in the present (the resurrected Christ in the midst of his people, the reign of God in the celebration of the Eucharist). Moreover, in popular culture, words like "apocalyptic" have taken on whole other meanings. Apocalypse is now probably more associated with zombies than with Jesus.

But Christians think about the end because it orients our lives now. One of the most sustained treatises on this end is the final book of the Bible, Revelation. There, we find an astonishing vision.

Christian Unity before God

If you know anything about Revelation, you might know of its references to the four horsemen of the apocalypse, great battles, a dragon, and a lot more that can strain the imagination. But even those visions can't touch what is described in the seventh chapter: "a great multitude that no one could count, from every nation, from all tribes and peoples and languages, standing before the throne and before the Lamb. . . . They cried out in a loud voice, saying, 'Salvation belongs to our God who is seated on the throne, and to the Lamb!'" (Revelation 7:9–10).

If you have ever experienced parish life, you will know just how unbelievable this is: a whole company of Christians united in a single task, the praise of God. Many congregations have enough trouble deciding what hymns to sing, how to arrange the pews, or what kind of coffee to have at fellowship hour. And most church folks come from relatively similar backgrounds. In Revelation, the vast multitude is drawn from a huge array of cultures, and they are all oriented in the same direction: to God and God's Son.

Revelation was written in a specific time and place. The author was not planning to offer a coherent picture of how the world would end. But the vision of Christian unity says a lot about both the purpose and conclusion of the actions God began in Creation. First, the end—in both senses—of human existence is union with all God's followers in worship of God. Revelation was written in Greek, so it does not use these words, but this vision describes *shalom* and *ḥesed*. People are united across boundaries of difference, which means the horizontal relationship is restored; and they are united in praise of God, which means the vertical relationship is restored.

Second, the vision in Revelation shows us what our life to come—what the church calls everlasting life—is like. The passage matches the definition of everlasting life in the Episcopal catechism: the moment when "we are united with all the people of God, in the joy of fully knowing and loving God and each other" (BCP, 862).

Finally, the end involves the return of Christ. Rather than coming to earth in a manger in a backwater corner of a major empire, Christ will return, as we affirm in the Nicene Creed, "in glory."

One word that describes this vision of the end is **fulfillment**. God created a world of *shalom* and *hesed*. God restored that world in Christ. In the end, God will act to fulfill the abundance of life that is offered in Christ's resurrection so that it pervades all creation. The Nicene Creed calls this "the life of the world to come," the time when all people will participate in that risen life of the reign of God. When the creed talks of "the resurrection of the dead," it is referring to that moment when our own lives and our lives as members of Christian communities will be finally fulfilled in a new kind of existence in Christ.

The belief in a final fulfillment takes us back to the affirmation that opens the creed: God is Creator, not a destroyer. However popular culture otherwise portrays it, Revelation ends not with destruction but with a vision of a new Jerusalem coming down to earth. This is the eschatological vision of Christians: a new Jerusalem in which we are finally one with one another and with God. It is here that we find our end.

Left Behind?

There have been many vivid and colorful interpretations of eschatology throughout history. Over the centuries, communities in distress have found comfort in these apocalyptic passages, which is fitting since a community suffering under the Roman Empire was the likely original audience for Revelation. But some interpretations verge on the fanciful. The **Rapture**, for instance, the belief that some people will be suddenly taken to heaven, has developed only recently in Christian history and has scant biblical grounding. Yet it has proven so influential, many people associate it with basic Christian teaching, and bookshelves blossom with best-selling novels about the end times.

Well-meaning efforts to reason about what happens after loved ones die have led to elaborate beliefs about heaven and hell, often with only the barest connection to what Jesus himself said. When the Bible speaks about the end, it is primarily about the fulfillment of new life. Heaven in the form of the new Jerusalem comes to earth, not vice versa.

Tied into these differing views is the idea of "the last judgment." Episcopalians affirm in the creed that when Christ returns in glory, he will "judge the living and the dead." **Judgment** is a word—like sin or repentance—that has acquired negative connotations. Better, some might say, to dispense with it all together.

We can't dispense with judgment, however, because judgment is all around us. Often, we judge ourselves. We think we're too fat, too slow, not cool enough to be with the right crowd, not clever enough to succeed in the world. In graduate school, I often heard people talk about "imposter syndrome," the crippling self-judgment that made people think the school made a mistake admitting them. At the same time, we are constantly judging one another, a practice that leaves us a long way from the merciful love of God. We unjustly exclude one another, fail to recognize our connectedness, and do not respond to situations of desperate need in the world. Each of us is involved in judging ourselves and judging others, and our judgments are often misjudgments.

In this context, Christ's "last judgment" is good news. It is a final setting right of our misjudgments, and it only makes sense in light of all that we have seen of the merciful love of God. In the last judgment, we will understand ourselves as beloved, forgiven, and transformed, worthy of membership in the reign of God. In rendering judgment on the world's misdealings and injustices, God will set all relationships aright. The last judgment opens space for the *shalom* and *hesed* of the kingdom to finally be fully known.

Hope, Not Fear

The particular trouble with ornate eschatological beliefs is not that they are only loosely based in the Bible; it is that they provide little nourishment for the journey of faith. If we are constantly wondering whether we are "Rapture ready," we may not be oriented towards seeking reconciliation with all of God's children on earth. If we are worried about a "last judgment" that will condemn us to hell, our lives may be dominated by fear, an emotion that is rarely productive or constructive.

Rather than fear or uncertainty, the virtue most closely associated with Christian eschatology is **hope**. Christian hope stands in between two other stances that are common in our time.

First, hope is not optimism. Techno-entrepreneurs and TED-talkers thrive on optimism. They insist that if we could just listen to their data-driven solutions, we could resolve a world of problems and live a better life. But Christians know the reality of human imperfection and frailty. We are not so naïve as to believe that suddenly humans will become perfect creations on our own.

Neither is hope—obviously—cynicism. Cynicism equally pervades our society, corroding discourse and relationships. Cynicism acts as if it is the only practical response to the way the world really works, and that hope is naïve. Actually, hope is based in what God has already done in the world in Jesus Christ. It is also rooted in our present reality of new life in Christ.

Hope is, as the catechism says, living "with confidence in newness and fullness of life" and "await[ing] the coming of Christ in glory and the completion of God's purpose for the world" (BCP, 861). God will fulfill what has been made real in

Christ's resurrection. As we enter that life in baptism and Eucharist, we are led into the confidence that God will fulfill and finally realize God's own kingdom.

It is right to associate hope with confidence, a word that literally means "with faith." Hope is living with faith in God. That hope does not make us passive and quiescent. It makes us active, engaged, and even impatient. Our hope for the final fulfillment makes us impatient with the shortcomings in our own lives and in the world. This returns us to mission. Mission is a hope-driven activity oriented to the world that God is unveiling. Hope drives us to bring the Eucharist into the world and help more people to glimpse the kingdom in their midst. Christian action is an expression of Christian hope. Rather than fear, Christian eschatology leads to hope and to mission.

When Is the End?

No matter how fervent and impatient our hope, it does not answer the burning question in most eschatological discussion: when? When will this fulfillment happen? Throughout history, different Christian groups have been convinced they would see Christ's return in their own time. We are still waiting.

But God's sense of time is not our own. If Adam and Eve were the ones who initiated our fall from God's Creation, why did it take God so long to send Christ to redeem the world? And if Christ came to redeem the world, why was he Incarnate as a helpless baby, who had to "waste" the first thirty years of his life before he began his ministry?

Instead of answering *when* God will fulfill Creation, Episcopalians can say that we live in an **in-between time**: God has restored *shalom* and *hesed* in Christ, but not all Creation has been ushered into the resurrection life. The Eucharist embodies this in-betweenness. We get a glimpse of the coming kingdom and are sent into a church and a world that is not yet perfected in God's wholeness.

In this in-between place, Christians can offer a foretaste of what is coming. Because Christians know what the end looks like—we see it every time we celebrate the Eucharist—we can live now like the end is here. When we live in the Eucharistic community as people who have died and risen with Christ, when we are at peace with God and one another, then we are experiencing a foretaste of what is to come. If you ask an Episcopalian *when* the end will come, we respond both, "It's right here, in our midst!" and "Look, it's still coming in all its glory."

Saints Among Us

Some Christians, both in the past and in our own time, have lived in this in-between time with particular grace. We call these people **saints**. Some were great missionaries, scholars, monks, nuns, bishops, lay people, or activists. The Episcopal Church has a whole list of people whom we commemorate throughout the year as saints. But you don't have to be famous or on this list to be a saint. In addition to the church's calendar of saints, I keep a personal calendar that includes people who have shaped my faith and pointed me towards God's future, like a summer camp director or a Sunday School teacher.

Saints are not saints because they are perfect people. None of them were. They are saints because their lives pointed beyond their current existence. They demonstrated the way to the life of *shalom* and *hesed*, a whole, full, and reconciled way begun in Creation, restored in Christ, and to be fulfilled by God. When we celebrate the Eucharist, our communion is not only with God and one another, but with this panoply of saints who have pointed us towards God and God's love. In joining the life of our Christian communities, saints remind us of the answer to the *when* question: now and not yet. This is the space where Christian living and Christian mission happen.

TO PONDER

- What do you think of when you hear the word "apocalypse"?

- How does Christian eschatology help shape our lives of faith now?

- Who have been the saints in your life?

Conclusion

There is a prayer at the beginning of the Eucharist service that always grabs my attention. It begins, "Almighty God, to you all hearts are open, all desires known, and from you no secrets are hid" (BCP, 355). If you take this seriously, it is a scary proposition. There have been times in my life when things I would rather have kept hidden—who I had a crush on in middle school, for instance, or how ineptly I sing karaoke—have been brought into public view. The results have been mortifying and shaming. Knowledge is power, and there is knowledge about myself I would be happy to keep hidden.

Beyond embarrassment, there are more significant matters at stake. I am intimately acquainted with my own failings and inability to live as God is calling me to. I know how thoroughly ungraceful I can be, how I can be an obstacle to the kingdom Jesus preached. And God, this prayer asserts, knows it. You call this good news?

That is the claim Christians have been making for two thousand years. God's love for the world—for me, for you, for all people, and for all Creation—is a personal, intimate, knowing love. God became human in Jesus Christ, took on the worst of the world's brokenness—death—and defeated it. God knows the depths of our failings. And rather than that knowledge being an opportunity for power over us or for shame or embarrassment, for God it is an opportunity for love. God sees us in our sin and offers a merciful love that invites us to participate in a new and abundant life. Rather than having to hide, we open to God and say, "Here, help me be your new creation."

Paul came to a similar point in his first letter to the Corinthians. After a lengthy teaching about the nature of community, the body of Christ, and the centrality of *agape*, he writes, "Now I know only in part; then I will know fully, even as I have been fully known" (13:12). It is an astonishing admission from the man who is one of the great originators of Christian theology. Even Paul's ideas about God are only partial and incomplete. But what is clear to Paul is that he has been *fully known*. There was much that Paul might have wanted to keep secret from God. But his heart, his desires, his secrets are open to God. Paul rests confidently in God's knowledge of him because he knows he has been transformed by this love. That transformation freed him to be a missionary and a theologian.

Christian theology is not done by perfect people. It is not done by people who completely "get it." Rather, theology is for people who are willing to let themselves be fully known, people who understand God's love embraces their imperfections, people who are willing to let that love begin to transform them into new creations. This is where our journey as theologians begins.

Amen

In the introduction, I summarized the content of the gospel in the length of a tweet: "You are loved with a love unlike any else that leads to a life unlike any else—now go, show that love & life to others. #grace #gospel." Being fully known by God is a love unlike any else. In this love, we are invited to participate in the abundant life of the reign of God. In baptism we are adopted into this life; in the Eucharist we see this richness of life; in mission we invite others to join us even as we look towards God's final fulfillment.

Whether in the length of a tweet or the length of a book, it is important to understand what Christians believe, why we believe it, and how we express and live it. It helps us communicate credibly in a world that is constantly challenging assertions and questioning authority. It gives us material to help talk to friends, family, colleagues, and even strangers about Jesus.

This sounds challenging, and it should be. Not only is it difficult to approach others in the same open, humble, receptive, and fearless spirit that Jesus demonstrated, but theology itself is not neat and tidy. In presenting the Christian faith in a series of short chapters, this book might be giving the wrong impression. God's love for the world cannot be contained by our human minds, and certainly not by our human words. Just when Jesus's followers thought they understood him as Messiah, he was crucified. Just when they were coming to terms with that death, he rose again. Just when we think we have "gotten" it, God tends to do something new in our lives that makes us see God's love in newer, more profound ways. It is why the journey of Christian living and Christian theology is ever evolving. No matter how mature we may grow in the faith, God is calling us to grow still more.

There is a short word that Episcopalians append to the Nicene Creed and use at several other points in the liturgy: *Amen*. It's originally a Hebrew word, but it has been so grafted into the life of Christian communities that it is hard sometimes to remember what it even means.

Amen means something like, "This is true" or "So be it." But that doesn't capture the full force of the word. We are affirming that these words in the creed, the prayers, and much more, are simply, powerfully, wonderfully true. The vision that is captured in the Nicene Creed of a loving, saving, sending God embodies this deep truth.

Reasoning about God—theology—does not end with reciting the creed. It does not end with reading books. It ends when that *Amen* comes to pervade our lives and the life of the world. It ends when we allow God to speak and work through us so that our *Amen* comes to be true in our daily lives.

So be it. May God's invitation to participate in a reign of *shalom* and *ḥesed* pervade the world. So be it. May Jesus Christ be known in and through us. So be it. May the Holy Spirit blow us in directions we can only begin to imagine. So be it. May we live the new life of baptism. So be it. May our churches be communities of mission that practice reconciliation in the world around them. So be it.

Since Pentecost, God's Spirit has been blowing the members of the church in hopeful and wonder-filled directions. When we open ourselves to be fully known by God, when we say "Amen" to the love and life offered in God's reign, when we take the ancient understandings of our faith and apply them to our modern context, we can be confident that God will be calling us to a richness and wholeness of life we can only begin to imagine. It is what God has always done.

TO PONDER

- Try again: how would you summarize the gospel or good news in 140 characters, the length of a tweet?
- Look again at the Nicene Creed: which parts do you see in a new light after reading this book?

Additional Resources

The Nicene Creed

We believe in one God,
    the Father, the Almighty,
    maker of heaven and earth,
    of all that is, seen and unseen.

We believe in one Lord, Jesus Christ,
    the only Son of God,
    eternally begotten of the Father,
    God from God, Light from Light,
    true God from true God,
    begotten, not made,
    of one Being with the Father.
    Through him all things were made.
    For us and for our salvation
      he came down from heaven:
by the power of the Holy Spirit
    he became incarnate from the Virgin Mary,
    and was made man.

For our sake he was crucified under Pontius Pilate;
   he suffered death and was buried.
   On the third day he rose again
     in accordance with the Scriptures;
   he ascended into heaven
     and is seated at the right hand of the Father.
He will come again in glory to judge the living and the dead,
   and his kingdom will have no end.

We believe in the Holy Spirit, the Lord, the giver of life,
   who proceeds from the Father and the Son.
   With the Father and the Son he is worshiped and glorified.
   He has spoken through the Prophets.
   We believe in one holy catholic and apostolic Church.
   We acknowledge one baptism for the forgiveness of sins.
   We look for the resurrection of the dead,
     and the life of the world to come. Amen.

(BCP, 326–327)

Further Reading

The Episcopal and Anglican tradition has long emphasized the teachings of the "early church," the first several centuries of Christian theology. Three books that help introduce a general audience to some of the wide diversity of thinking in this period are:

- Henry Chadwick, *The Early Church*, 1967/1993
- Robert Louis Wilken, *The Spirit of Early Christian Thought*, 2003
- Rowan Williams, *Silence and Honey Cakes*, 2004

Over five centuries, the Anglican and Episcopal churches have produced a wide array of gifted men and women who have reflected theologically on various aspects of the Christian faith. A very small selection includes:

- Richard Hooker, *Of the Laws of Ecclesiastical Polity*, 1594
- Lancelot Andrewes, *Private Devotions*, 1675
- Richard Baxter, *The Reformed Pastor*, 1656
- Frederick D. Maurice, *The Kingdom of Christ*, 1838
- Evelyn Underhill, *Mysticism*, 1911
- Michael Ramsey, *The Gospel and the Catholic Church*, 1936
- John Stott, *Basic Christianity*, 1959
- William Stringfellow, *An Ethic for Christians and Other Aliens in a Strange Land*, 1973
- Rowan Williams, *Resurrection: Interpreting the Easter Gospel*, 1982

More recent books designed to explain the faith to a general audience of Anglicans and Episcopalians include:

- Mark McIntosh, *Mysteries of Faith,* 2000
- Kathryn Tanner, *Jesus, Humanity and the Trinity*, 2001

- Rowan Williams, *Tokens of Trust*, 2007
- Samuel Wells, *What Episcopalians Believe: An Introduction*, 2011
- Sarah Coakley, *God, Sexuality, and Self*, 2013
- Tom Wright, *Simply Good News*, 2015